FRANCIS OF ASSISI
AND POWER

Jacques Dalarun

Francis of Assisi and Power

Franciscan Institute Publications
The Franciscan Institute
Saint Bonaventure University
Saint Bonaventure, NY   14778
2007

Original title:
François d'Assise ou le pouvoir en question
© De Boeck & Larcier s.a., Département De Boeck Université
Paris, Bruxelles, 1999

Cover illustration:
Francis of Assisi appearing during the Chapter in Arles,
Middle of 14th century

Cover design: Mark Sullivan

Library of Congress Cataloging-in-Publication Data

Dalarun, Jacques.
    [Françoise d'Assise. English]
    Francis of Assisi and power / Jacques Dalarun.
        p. cm. -- (Franciscan Institute publications)
    Includes bibliographical referrences and index.
    ISBN 978-1-57659-142-0 (alk. paper)
    1. Franciscans--Government. 2. Francis, of Assisi, Saint, 1182-1226. I. Title.
    BX3604.4.D3513 2007
    255'.3--dc22

                                2007003231

Printed in the United States of America
BookMasters, Inc.
Ashland, Ohio
USA

CONTENTS

Abbreviations

Writings of Francis

Adm	The Admonitions
CtC	The Canticle of the Creatures
ER	The Earlier Rule (Regula Non Bullata)
LR	The Later Rule (Regula Bullata)
LtMin	A Letter to a Minister
LtOrd	A Letter to the Entire Order
1LtCus	The First Letter to the Custodians
2LtCus	The Second Letter to the Custodians
2LtF	The Second Letter to the Faithful
RH	Rule for Hermitages
SalV	Salutation of Virtues
Test	The Testament
TPJ	True and Perfect Joy

Franciscan Sources

AP	The Anonymous of Perugia
LMj	The Major Legend by Bonaventure
LP	The Legend of Perugia
L3C	The Legend of the Three Companions
1C	The Life of St. Francis by Thomas of Celano
2C	The Remembrance of the Desire of a Soul by Thomas of Celano
3C	The Treatise on the Miracles by Thomas of Celano

Biblical Sources

1 Cor	1 Corinthians	Lk	Luke
Acts	Acts of the Apostles	Lv	Leviticus
Ex	Exodus	Mt	Matthew
Gal	Galatians	Nm	Numbers
Jn	John	Prv	Proverbs

PREFACE

The present volume was first published in French: *François d'Assise ou le pouvoir en question* in the series "Bibliothèque du Moyen Âge" (Paris–Brussels: De Boeck Université, 1999). It was, in the author's own words, the third volume of Jacques Dalarun's Franciscan trilogy. After publishing *The Misadventure of Francis of Assisi* in 2002, and *Francis of Assisi and the Feminine* in 2006, Franciscan Institute Publications now has the pleasure to publish *Francis of Assisi and Power*.

Our gratitude goes to Anne Bartol, OSC for patiently and carefully working with us on the English translation of the original French text. We are also thankful to Roberta McKelvie, OSF and Daria Mitchell, OSF for reviewing and editing the text. We also congratulate Daria for laying out this book. And, last but not least, we want to express a special thanks to our colleague, Robert J. Karris, OFM for his meticulous proofreading and the valuable suggestions he brought to greatly improve this publication.

Jean François Godet-Calogeras, Ph.D.
Editor

FOREWORD

The present volume is the third and final installment in a trilogy of works on selected aspects of the Franciscan movement originally published in Italian or French by the renowned French medievalist, Jacques Dalarun. With this volume we bring to a satisfying conclusion the collaborative venture between Professor Dalarun and the Franciscan Institute that began with the publication of the first of these three volumes in 2002.

In that first volume, *The Misadventure of Francis of Assisi*, Professor Dalarun examined the evolution of the different portrayals of Francis of Assisi in a variety of narrative texts, spanning approximately thirty-five years, from the *Vita prima* of Thomas of Celano (1229) to the *Legenda maior* of Bonaventure of Bagnoregio (1263). He characterizes this journey, however, as a "misadventure" (*una malavventura*) – the sad, almost regrettable eclipsing of the complexities of the historical Francis by the more stereotypical and theologized portraits of the hagiographical Francis. In the process, he says, the more attractive Francis – the one who compels our attention and respect because he appears more real, more human (and even more flawed) like the rest of us – came to be lost in favor of a portrayal in which he has been transformed into a symbol of the perfectly virtuous Christian life. Francis, in such portrayals, may be worthy of our admiration but not identification, still less our imitation.

The second volume, *Francis of Assisi and the Feminine*, ventured onto very different terrain: namely, the question of Francis's relationship not only with women (most notably Clare of Assisi) but more profoundly with those broader trends towards what might be called the feminization of religion that were occurring in the central Middle Ages. Dalarun has typified the place of Francis in this transformation of the traditional expressions of religious experience as *"un passagio"* – a kind of transitional point in a much wider phenomenon. Francis, in other words, stands as it were between the bold experiment of Robert of Arbrissel at Fontevraud in the early 12th century (in which men subjected themselves to the authority of women as the supreme act of penitence) and Clare of Rimini who in the early 14th century sought to claim in her pronouncements a rightful place for women in the arena of Christian spirituality. Francis, in other words, had been both influenced by and was influential upon this profound cultural shift. And the primary stage for this dynamic interplay was none other than his complex and often-misunderstood relationship with Clare.

This third volume, the slimmest but perhaps the most provocative of the three, now treats the question of power and authority in the life and writings of Francis and even more expansively in the troubled events of the history of the Order of Friars Minor during the first fifty years of its existence. Building upon the magisterial treatment of the subject by Rosalind B. Brooke in 1959,[1] Dalarun goes well beyond – one might even say underneath – this earlier landmark study. For not only had a number of important textual fragments dealing with the subject of how authority was structured in the Franciscan Order come

---

[1] Rosalind B. Brooke, *Early Franciscan Government: From Elias to Bonaventure* (Cambridge: Cambridge University Press, 1959).

to light during the intervening years,[2] but historians had also developed a more critical approach to the wide array of sources which serve as the basis of our knowledge of the events of early Franciscan history.[3]

The common thread connecting all three volumes – indeed, the concern that motivates and shapes Dalarun's most important contributions to Franciscan scholarship – is the absolute centrality of the question of sources: the reading, interpreting and use of the sources at the disposal of the historian. *The Misadventure* is, in fact, all about sources and the critical importance of distinguishing or sorting out history from hagiography, fact from model or template. Hence: it is not just a matter of having sources to work with – scholars of the Franciscan phenomenon are blessed with an embarrassment of riches in this regard by comparison with many other religious traditions – but of reading them critically and correctly.

The arguments presented in *Francis of Assisi and the Feminine* are likewise built upon a careful examination of the sources: the author studies over four hundred references in the sources to the thematic being traced. Here, the reader is called upon to widen the parameters of his or her investigative canvas, contextualizing the source materials for the Franciscan story within the framework of the broader religious and cultural movements of

---

[2] Most notably by Cesare Cenci concerning the constitutions issued at the momentous General Chapter of 1239 which shed important light on the work that had traditionally (prior to Brooke) been attributed to Bonaventure in his Constitutions of Narbonne of 1260.

[3] It should be remembered that Brooke produced her study before the latest renaissance in Franciscan studies that occurred from the late 1960s forward, much of it largely due to those scholars associated, Raoul Manselli in the lead, with the revival of Paul Sabatier's *Società internazionale di studi francescani* in Assisi.

the day. In other words, "source" is not only text but context.

Both of these elements now converge in the present volume. Indeed, the driving energy behind the forceful, often vehement (and sometimes even potentially offensive) presentation of the thesis found in *Francis of Assisi and Power* is precisely the lack of attention to and respect for the sources when the problematic of Francis and his movement comes to be examined by historians. Such scholars, Dalarun insists, have a disturbing tendency to see in the sources the Francis they want to see or prefer to see or think they see there on the page. They thus too often engage in what biblical experts call eisegesis rather than exegesis: reading themselves into the sources (their own values and prejudices) rather than reading out of the sources what is actually there. The result of this inability to get beyond one's own prejudices or pre-judgments about Francis is, according to our author, yet another instance of the *malavventura* that surrounds the historical personage of the Poverello, robbing him (and us) of the rich, contradictory and complex person who lived, grew, changed, sinned, failed and struggled with himself, his brothers, his Church and even the papacy on his journey through life.

It is indeed a sad commentary that in spite of the evolution of the tools of critical scholarship over the last century (and particularly over the last decades), generations of historians have still been unable to properly disentangle – that is to say, to conceptually distinguish – the Francis who lived as a concrete historical person from the one who, shortly after his death in 1226, will be officially canonized as a saint in the Roman Church and then written about as one from 1228 onward. This one historiographical datum, Dalarun contends

– the perception of Francis as a saint and all that such a designation implies for the historian (and lay reader alike) – all-too-often impinges on the historian's ability to make proper assessments and judgments about the sources: respecting their chronology and their context, identifying their genre and their typologies, sifting through multiple and often conflicting viewpoints, evaluating the weight of the manuscript evidence, etc. And such inattention (or worse: such ingrained biases) ends up distorting the data that is under one's eyes in order to fit one's pre-conceived assumptions. Being the careful historian that he is, such critical sloppiness inevitably exasperates, leading occasionally to a certain stridency of tone.

The subject under discussion in this third volume – the understanding and use of power by Francis and his friars – therefore doubles back on and is one of the most vivid examples of the theme of the first volume: how does one use the sources to tell the historical and the meta-historical stories about the Franciscan phenomenon. Failure to distinguish the first from the second inevitably results in a considerably skewed version of events and issues which might accord well with the pre-conceived notions about Francis that the reader prefers to see in the sources but, in the long run, does a serious injustice to the reality of the person that one wants to understand. The facts, in other words, have not been allowed to tell their own story.

And from the point of view of our author, the question of power presents a perfect illustration of this persistent and nagging malady. In this brief but dense presentation before us, it is not the question of poverty that holds center stage as the cause of the controversies within the early fraternity as it moves out into history after the death of the founder. Rather, paradoxically, it is the question of his humility that becomes the nub issue, particularly with respect to how historians have read and interpreted those hagiographical attestations to his humility. Historians, he avers, begin with their own assumptions about what the humility of a saint should look like – behavior more akin to what we might call meekness or piety – and then assume this is how the humble Francis must have acted. However, in starting from such assumptions, historians are prevented from seeing what the texts – Francis's writings, the evidence from the chronicles, the hagiographical accounts themselves, even the legislation – tell us what happened both before and after 1226. Indeed, our author contends that the turmoil that arose over the question of power and authority in the Order after the death of Francis is actually rooted in Francis's own struggles with the very same question and the fact that he never resolved it during his own lifetime neither within himself nor within the Order that he founded.

This is why the author places such great weight – correctly, I believe – on the events surrounding what can be called the Emergency Chapter of 29 September 1220.[4] Here, a great confrontation took place between Francis and a growing number of clerics over the specific contours and directions which the fraternity was starting to take (and would take) in the years ahead. For what was at issue

---

[4] Professor Dalarun does not attempt in this volume a definitive resolution of the conflicting accounts of these events and the precise time in which some or all of them may have occurred. My own work on these events has led me to believe that Francis's confrontation with the clerics, his resignation and what the sources refer to as the Chapter of Mats all occurred at that same moment, namely, the extraordinary Chapter called by Francis, shortly after his return from the Holy Land, at the time which would have normally been reserved for Provincial Chapters: September 29, 1220.

can be briefly summarized in this way: were the friars to become a bona fide religious order within the Church, following one of the traditional rules and oriented towards apostolic usefulness as desired by the hierarchy and as championed by those friars trained in the clerical culture of the time; or was it to remain an evangelical leaven for the Church, living in relative obscurity among the *minores* of society, at a certain distance from the tumult and temptations of the new urban culture and following the distinctive *forma vitae* that had been developed by Francis and his early companions? The confrontation was bitter and brutal, resulting ultimately in the resignation – an act of humility, Celano tells us – of the founder. And yet, as Dalarun rightly insists, this was hardly the end of the story. Francis may have given up the function and title of minister general (such as it was at the time), and yet he continued to act in ways as if he were still "the minister and servant of all the friars." Indeed, not only did he, at this point, take up the pen and begin to write to the friars (something he had not done up to that time) as a means of continuing to influence the friars in their way of life. But he also seemed to continue to act as if he were still minister general, even after he had appointed Peter Catania (September 1220) and then Elias of Cortona (May 1221) to serve as minister in his stead. For, as the author points out, it was Francis (and not Elias), at least according to the sources available to us, who almost single-handedly hammered out the definitive rule with Ugolino and the curial canonists between 1221 and 1223.[5] Francis, in other words, may have given up power but he surely never surrendered his authority within the community, as evidenced by the

---

[5] The appearance of the word *ego* no less than eight times in the Rule of 1223 refers, of course, to Francis himself – a rather strange formulation given the public resignation of Francis in late 1220.

last dying gasp of his Testament which he expected to be copied, read, heeded and obeyed.

But this is precisely where Dalarun finds Francis so troubling and so contradictory. He gave up power to others only to yet keep it and cling to it himself. He wrote and talked about the merits of the surrender of power[6] without being able to live it out when it came his turn to do so. And in the process, his language became more embittered and his call for punishments to be levied on those who would not heed him more frequent and shrill. So much, our author chides, for the humble Francis!

This inability to resolve the question of power and authority within himself and thereby within the life of the early fraternity will, however, be the seed for what is to follow over the next forty years of Franciscan history. This connection between Francis and Franciscan history is what eludes most historians; and such is one of the great merits of Dalarun's presentation. This is why he structures much of what is to follow around the events of the four General Chapters where the issues of power came to be heatedly argued about and only rarely resolved with any definitive answers: (1) the Emergency (or Extraordinary) Chapter of 1220 which ends with the resignation of Francis; (2) the Chapter of 1230 in Assisi in which the Testament is declared to have no juridical authority over the life of the friars and where the precedent is set of inviting the papacy – in the person of Ugolino / Gregory IX – to help the friars resolve their thorny and divisive issues; (3) the General Chapter of 1239 in Rome which saw an open revolt spearheaded mainly by ultramontane Franciscans (from Paris, Germany and England) against

---

[6] Perhaps the clearest references are Admonitions 4, 19 and also 14.

the central authority of the Order and which led to the deposition of Brother Elias of Cortona and the formulation of constitutions intended for the "reform of the whole Order;" and finally (4) the General Chapter of 1260 in Narbonne where Bonaventure – the general minister who had replaced yet another deposed minister, John of Parma – reorganized and codified the legislation growing within the Order since the tumultuous Chapter of 1239 in the justly famous Constitutions of Narbonne.

In this tight but grand survey, Dalarun points out how the friars, in multiple different experiments, tried to resolve the question of how power was to be structured or shared out within the community; how to balance, as it were, central authority and local autonomy; and how different friars in different places at different times differed on what that ought to look like. Like the famous pendulum, the concrete answer announced at any given time varied from period to period, context to context – be it in 1239 or the Chapter of Definitors in 1241; be it in the Exposition of the Four Masters, the Rule Commentary of Hugh of Digne or the pseudo-Bonaventurean Commentary on the Rule. The friars of different cultural backgrounds and different experiences of the use of power were simply trying to get it right. But, as Dalarun contends, the fact that the founder himself had never gotten it right for himself sowed the very seeds of this discord for decades to come.

Hence, this volume represents a real *tour de force* of the medieval sources dealing with the question of power among the Franciscans. Our author deftly dissects these sources, laying bare the struggles, the contradictions, the diverse positions held within the Order and the nuances in these efforts to get it right. Never before has the problem of how power came to be structured in the

Order of Friars Minor been so closely examined with all the different permutations laid out for our viewing.

There are, however, two other elements which can be added to this masterful study which might serve as a complement to the data already contained within this provocative volume. Both, it seems to me, would help to clarify a little further *why* the issue of power and authority came to be such an issue within the Franciscan movement in the first place during the early decades of its existence.

Even though Professor Dalarun explains within the first pages of his monograph that his intention is not to discuss the wider social dynamics of the question of power in medieval society and its effects upon the Franciscan phenomenon,[7] it is nonetheless imperative to understanding Francis's own sensitivity to how power was used (and abused) in society and the Church (and, by extension within the Order itself) in relationship to these very same dynamics. There is, in other words, a question of power within Francis and the early fraternity because there is a question about how power was used (and abused) outside the Order. For Francis was keenly aware not only of the various forms of power that were operative in Assisian society (e.g., money, military force, ownership of land and property, class consciousness, learning and so forth) but most especially of how that power came to be used to the detriment of its weakest members: the poor. This cardinal insight was due, of

---

[7] This is, in fact, a subject treated to some extent by myself in the first chapter of my doctoral dissertation, cited by our author in the first footnote of his presentation. That first chapter covers Francis and the dynamics of the early minorite fraternity. Cf. M. Cusato, *La renonciation au pouvoir chez les Frères Mineurs au 13e siècle* (Diss. PhD., Université de Paris IV – Sorbonne, 1991).

course, to his famous encounter one day with lepers: an encounter which became for him the prism through which he would henceforth view all of life and reality, including his own. He saw how power could wreak havoc in human life and society but also knew that the locus for those impulses – so difficult to tame – were within the human heart.

Moreover, it was precisely when the early fraternity began to grow and expand – most notably when the Chapter of 1217 sent the friars on mission northward over the mountains and overseas to the Holy Land – that it became readily apparent that more formal structures of order and authority were required for the well-being of the brothers and the integrity of their *forma vitae*, lest the whole enterprise be jeopardized by unclarity, instability and even religious anarchy. It was at this very point that the friars were obliged to develop their own structures of authority – ministers, custodes, provinces, chapters, etc. – but always with an eye to how power ought (and ought not) be used by the friars among the friars as distinct from how they knew power was all-too-often used out in society, by the Church at large and even within other religious orders. In the famous words of the Gospel text cited in this regard in the Early Rule: "'it shall not be that way among' the friars."[8]

The social dynamics of power tell us something about the sources for the sensitivity to the question of power within Francis and his early friars. But a second element is necessary to understand why Francis clung so tenaciously to power during his last years after his alleged resignation. Professor Dalarun, in some of his most alarming paragraphs, depicts Francis at this point in

---

[8] " ... *non sic erit inter fratres.*" (RNB 5).

his life as alternately contradictory, incoherent, arrogant, egotistical and megalomaniacal: in short, a deeply conflicted person when it comes to his apparent inability to truly surrender the reins of power within the Order. And yet, might there not be another explanation for this profound interior battle within the soul of the Poverello – one that might perhaps be more understanding of the man and his dilemma? For what seems absent from the presentation before us is an understanding of what was truly at stake for Francis after 1220: namely, the survival of the way of life (the *forma vitae*) which he and his friars had carefully and strenuously hammered out over many years, believing themselves under the guidance of the Spirit and in consonance with the life and values of Jesus of Nazareth in the Gospels. This evangelical form of life, this call to do penance which often implied a life at odds with the ways of communal and ecclesiastical Assisi, was perceived to be under direct and unwarranted attack – either through an honest lack of comprehension or a willful desire to adopt other more conventional forms of religious living. What Francis struggled to hold onto was not so much his office – which he more or less resigned – but the life which made sense of his own life and which, he believed, was what the Lord had led him and his brothers to offer the men and women of their own time. The ultimate effect of these struggles is the same: the questions about power within the Order were never definitively resolved during Francis's lifetime, setting the fraternity on its tempestuous journey through the early decades of the thirteenth century, as this volume so well charts and illustrates. But the motivation for this struggle and the reasons for the failure of Francis to actually resolve it appear rather different when the survival of the charism – the imperative of preserving intact the *forma vitae fratrum minorum* – is placed within the historical mix as the critical datum explaining the actions of the founder after his resignation. If Francis does not appear quite so humble as the hagiographers would have us believe nor as hubristic or egotistical as our author might wish to depict him, he does appear as a man of enormous passion struggling to remain faithful to – indeed, hold onto against all efforts to the contrary – a way of life whose ethical and spiritual content continues to speak to the hopes of men and women of all ages for a better, more peaceful and humane world.

The study which now follows thus represents a welcome and genuine breakthrough in the historiography of the Franciscan phenomenon in the Middle Ages. Although it closes a chapter in the collaboration between the members of the Franciscan Institute and Professor Dalarun, his more recent work on site at the Institute as the Fr. Joseph A. Doino, O.F.M. Visiting Professor of Franciscan Studies and especially his research with the resident faculty on the so-called Legend of the Three Companions opens the door to further avenues for an exciting and promising collaborative relationship and scholarly production in the years ahead.

Michael F. Cusato, O.F.M.
Director, Franciscan Institute

INTRODUCTION

Principles and Modes of Government
In the Order of Friars Minor

The greatest of social evils is power. The best definition of the abusive person is potens.[9]

For he [Elias] *had the whole Order in his power* [in sua potestate], *just as blessed Francis had had it and also Brother John Parenti who had preceded him.*[10]

Two citations. The first is from a contemporary historian, Jacques Le Goff; the second is from Jordan of Giano, Franciscan chronicler of the thirteenth century. Both apply to the same man, to the same Order – to Francis of Assisi and to the Order of Friars Minor, created at his instigation. Which of these two voices should we

---

[9] J. Le Goff, "Le vocabulaire des catégories sociales chez saint François d'Assise et ses biographes du XIIIe siècle," in *Ordres et classes. Colloque d'histoire sociale, Saint-Cloud 24-25 May 1967*, ed. D. Roche and C. E. Labrousse (Paris-La Haye, 1973), 118.

[10] Jordan of Giano, *Chronica fratris Jordani*, 61, ed. H. Boehmer, Paris (Collection d'études et de documents sur l'histoire religieuse et littéraire du Moyen Âge, 6), 1908; English translation in *Thirteenth Century Chronicles* (Chicago, 1961), 64. All English translations cited in this study were revised from the Latin texts.

believe? Did Francis harbor a hatred for power? Did he nevertheless exercise it in an absolute manner within his institution? Was this saint, so "popular" in every sense of the word,[11] also an autocrat? On the contrary, was he concerned about harmonizing his outreach to the most marginal of the society of his time with "democratic" forms of government within the community of his brothers?

To respond appropriately to this question would require the rewriting of a history of both Franciscan spirituality and of the Order of Friars Minor, a history which must also reflect accurately the evolution of religious institutes and the institutional Church against the unfolding of religious and secular events of the same era. To do so is not the aim of this study. The plan here is only to reread a few of the early Franciscan sources, which run from the beginnings to about 1260, with this question of power in mind. In this well-intentioned wandering, the gulf of anachronism threatens the walker at every step. It would certainly be extremely anachronistic to judge the Franciscan experience according to our contemporary systems of representative government. On the other hand, we will begin with the assumption that it offers us a parable on power which, even today, has not lost all its relevance.[12]

---

[11] A. Bartoli Langeli, "Le radici culturali della "popolarità" francescana," in *Il francescanesimo e il teatro medievale. Atti del convegno nazionale di studi, San Miniato, 8-9-10 ottobre 1982*, Castelfiorentino (Biblioteca della "Miscellanea storica della Valdelsa", 6), 1984, 41-58.

[12] For the general Franciscan bibliography: J. Dalarun, *The Misadventure of Francis of Assisi* (St. Bonaventure, 2002), 259-286; Id., *Francis of Assisi and the Feminine* (St. Bonaventure, 2006), 287-331; *Francesco d'Assisi e il primo secolo di storia francescana*, Turin (Biblioteca Einaudi 1), 1997, 377-425. The following pages include only citations of the sources used and the most directly applicable bibliography. I would like to express my gratitude here to two people: Claude Nicolet, who enkindled my curiosity for this subject when he invited me to

In its beginnings, the Order that is called "Franciscan," or more accurately "The Order of Friars Minor,"[13] was a fraternity of mostly lay individuals who decided to do penance. The founder, in his concern to live "according to the form of the Holy Gospel,"[14] chose to establish in a rule of religious life the condition shared by the most powerless classes in the society of his time: destitution, precariousness, itinerancy, manual labor. He showed a loathing for all forms of power that went far beyond the scorn of the world as found in the monastic and ascetic tradition.[15] With Francis, there is less of a merely visible break with the world; at the heart of his life there is instead more intransigence toward any compromise with the world and its powers. He accepted, seemingly with regret, the institutionalization of his experience, which, born in central Italy, is strictly contemporary with the blossoming of the communal regime at the moment in which it passed from its so-called "consular" and "ruling" phases. Both of these phases, which emanated from the factions of an urban aristocracy – evolved into a so-called "popular" phase. In this "popular" phase, the "arts" – the new trades – allowed access to political

---

speak on June 10, 1997 at his seminar of the E.P.H.E. (École Pratique des Hautes Études) (4th course), and Giulia Barone, who cleared up a number of confusing issues during a train journey from Spoleto to Rome on April 3, 1997.

[13] Afterwards, the adjective "Franciscan" will no longer be used except when speaking strictly of Francis himself, in order to avoid all unnecessary confusion between the founder and his foundation.

[14] Test 14. This work utilizes the Latin edition of François d'Assise, *Écrits*, ed. by T. Desbonnets, J.-F. Godet, T. Matura and D. Vorreux, Paris (Sources chrétiennes, 285), 1981.

[15] R. Bultot, *Christianisme et valeurs humaines. La doctrine du mépris du monde en Occident de saint Ambroise à Innocent III* (Paris, 1963-1964).

expression and governmental participation.[16] There is therefore some cause, not for asserting that Francis of Assisi was in any way the founder of modern democracy – the search for these origins being in itself absurd – but rather for wondering whether the radical stand of the Assisian faced with power had any influence on the determination of the governmental structures of the Order which he started and which claims to follow his teachings.

---

[16] P. Cammarosano, *Italia medievale. Struttura e geografia delle fonti scritte*, Rome (Studi superiori NIS, 109, Storia), 1991, 125-144.

Chapter One

From the Refusal of Power
To the Principles of a Government

Denial of Power

By designating power as "the greatest of social evils," Jacques Le Goff seized upon one of the driving forces of Franciscan thought. Indeed, an anthology could be drawn up of expressions not so much of hate for, as refusal of, power[1] in the writings of the man from Assisi:

> Blessed is the servant [*servus*] who does not think more highly of himself when he is praised and held in esteem by others than when he is held in contempt and thought to be vile and simple, for what a person is worth before God, that he is worth and no more. Cursed is the religious [*religioso*] who was raised to a high place by others and does not wish of his own will to come down. And blessed is this servant who is raised to a high

---

[1] This is the central theme of M. Cusato's thesis, *La renonciation au pouvoir chez les frères mineurs au 13e siècle*, dir. A. Vauchez, Paris-IV, 1991; I am very grateful to A. Vauchez for having told me about this remarkable work and hope that it will be published shortly.

place despite his wishes and who desires always to be under the feet of others.[2]

The *Admonitions,* from which this passage is an excerpt, is, after the *Testament* and the *Later Rule,* one of the most widely known Franciscan texts in the medieval tradition, present in the four large collections of manuscripts which preserve the writings of Francis for us and reproduced in fifty-eight copies.[3] Relying on the Gospel of Matthew,[4] the man from Assisi slides very quickly from a general message to an application specific to the religious life. He wastes no time railing against the world. This man, who would prefer meaningful action to empty words,[5] proposes another way of being, which today we would call an alternative model, and which, in his time, was simply called "conversion." It is thus within the context of the religious life, product of this radical conversion that is also a return to the evangelical source, that the overwhelming majority of expressions of the refusal of power lie. Thus, in the *Earlier Rule,* the older of the two preserved Franciscan *Rules,* there is naturally more written about the relationships internal to the community of friars:

And let none be called "prior [*prior*]," but let all generally be called "lesser brothers [*fratres minores*]." And let them wash each other's feet.[6]

---

[2] Adm 19.

[3] Cf. François d'Assise, *Écrits,* 9-13 and 23-47.

[4] Mt 24:46. All biblical citations are used with permission from the *New American Bible.*

[5] Adm 21.

[6] ER 6:3-4.

The image of the mutual washing of feet, on the theme of Holy Thursday,[7] recurs throughout the writings of Francis.[8] And it is again the Gospel, through its lexicon and structure, which irrigates a passage like this one:

> Likewise, let none of the brothers exercise any power or any form of domination [*potestatem vel dominationem*] in this way, especially among themselves. For, if the Lord says in the Gospel, "the rulers of the Gentiles lord it over them and the great ones [*maiores*] make their authority over them felt,"[9] it will not be this way among the brothers. And whoever will wish to become greater [*maior*] among them, let him be their minister and servant [*minister et servus*]. And let he who is greater [*maior*] among them become the least [*minor*].[10]

Indeed, according to Matthew, Christ had said:

> As for you, do not be called "Rabbi." You have but one teacher and you are all brothers. Call no one on earth your father; you have but one father in heaven. Do not be called "Master;" you have but one master, the Messiah. The greatest among you (*maior*) must be your servant (*minister*). Whoever exalts himself will be humbled, but whoever humbles himself will be exalted.[11]

---

[7] Here Jn 13:14.

[8] Adm 4:2-3; also the kissing of the feet in ER 24:3; 2LtF 87, LtOrd 12. M. Cusato, *La renonciation* ..., 113.

[9] Mt 20:25.

[10] ER 5:9-12. Cf. Mt 20:26-28.

[11] Mt. 23:8-12.

It is in Jesus' own life where Francis sees this teaching practiced, in this Incarnation of the Word whose acts speak more eloquently than words:

> And he was a poor man and a stranger, and he lived on alms, he and the Blessed Virgin and his disciples.[12]

On this delicate Gospel fabric, the man from Assisi embroiders new and original designs, as is seen in this excerpt from the *Salutation of the Virtues*:

> Holy Obedience confounds
> all bodily and carnal desires
> and keeps one mortified
> by obedience to the Spirit
> and by obedience to his brother;
> and he is subject to and under the command
> [*subditus et suppositus*]
> of all those who are in the world,
> and not only to people,
> but also to all the wild beasts
> [*omnibus bestiis et feris*],
> because they may do with him what they wish
> as far as it is granted to them by the Lord from on high.[13]

To have power over no one, to be subject to all: in this way must the anonymous member live, he who is defined only incidentally as the brother of his brother; in the evening of his life, this is what Francis wished for himself, as is seen in his *Testament:*

---

[12] ER 9:5.
[13] SalV 14-18.

And I firmly desire to obey the minister general of this fraternity [*ministro generali huius fraternitatis*] and any guardian that it pleases him to give me. And I wish to be held so firmly in his grasp that I would not be able to act without his permission and without his willing it, because he is my lord [*dominus meus*].[14]

Examples of this type of language abound in the Franciscan writings. The excerpts given here suffice to show that the total refusal to dominate, the equal willingness to be subject, the joy of humility, indeed, even an exultation in humiliation – so many attitudes brought to bear almost exclusively in the setting of the brothers' community – are the literal and radical application of the Gospel message, and include echoes of earlier monastic texts, such as Chapter VII of the *Rule* of Benedict of Nursia and the *Treatise on the Degrees of Humility* of Bernard of Clairvaux.[15]

Within this long-standing evangelical and ascetic tradition, the spirituality of Francis nevertheless stands out strongly, for at least four reasons. Francis lives the reversal that makes submission an almost absolute virtue in such a radical way that it becomes new: for example when he wishes the brother to be – and, probably, wishes to be himself – a subject of the wild beasts. "Minority"[16] is not one of many aspects of the Franciscan vocation – it is its very definition. There is no occasion in the writings of Francis when the high statutory importance of obedience and submission do not correspond clearly with his central theological principle: this descent, this

---

[14] Test 27-28.

[15] François d'Assise, *Écrits*, 358.

[16] The term "minority" is a convenient concept, but one which never appears as such in the Franciscan legends.

unheard-of abasement which was the Incarnation of God made man. And finally, if all the brothers are to live in this spirit and state of voluntary submission, those responsible for governing the others must be even more subject than the rest, in order to offset their apparent exalted status, and the most submissive of all must obviously be the founder.

The reversal culminates in *True and Perfect Joy*.[17] This text, well-known today, was for many years known only from the description given in the belated *Actus beati Francisci et sociorum eius,* a work of the early fourteenth century and the Latin model for the *Fioretti*. However, the original version, accepted as an authentic writing dictated by Francis to Brother Leo, was rediscovered in 1927 in a manuscript from the beginning of the fourteenth century:

> Write, he said, what is true joy. A messenger comes and says that all the masters of Paris have joined the order; write: this is not true joy. The same thing happens with all the prelates from across the mountains – bishops and archbishops – as well as the King of France and the King of England; write: this is not true joy. Likewise, if my brothers went among the Infidels and converted them all to the Faith, and if I have such grace from God that I cure the sick and perform many miracles, I tell you that in all this is not found true joy. What then is true joy? I return from Perugia and come here in the middle of the night; it is wintertime, muddy and so cold that icicles have formed along

---

[17] G. Miccoli, "A Christian Experience between Gospel and Institution," *Greyfriars Review* 11 (1997): 113-141; Id., "Gli scritti di Francesco," in *Francesco d'Assisi e il primo secolo di storia francescana,* 48-49.

the edge of my tunic and strike me continually on the legs, and blood flows from these wounds. And full of mud and cold and ice, I come to the door, and, after I have knocked and called out for a long time, a brother arrives who asks, "Who is it?" I respond, "Brother Francis." And he says: "Go away! This is not a decent hour to be walking about; you cannot come in." And, after I insist, he would respond again: "Go away! You're nothing but a simple-minded idiot; anyway, you are not coming in. We are fine here and certainly don't need you." And again, I remain at the door and say to him: "for the love of God, let me in tonight!" And he would answer: "I will not. Go to the Crosiers' place[18] and ask there!" I tell you, that if I remain patient and do not become upset, that in that is the true and perfect joy and the salvation of my soul.[19]

The legends dedicated to Francis of Assisi echo the message of the writings; they show explicitly the choice of minority, the understanding of the ministers' roles, and the paradoxical fate of the founder. This is shown in the *First Life,* composed in 1228-1229 and attributed to Thomas of Celano:

It is he [Francis] who in the beginning founded the Order of lesser brothers and here is the occasion when he gave them this name. As everyone knows, it is written in the *Rule*: "Let them be lesser

---

[18] See François d'Assise, *Écrits,* 121, note 2: "The Croisiers were instituted as a hospital order in Italy in 1169. In Francis' time, they ran a leper hospital, located mid-way between Assisi and the Portiuncula."

[19] TPJ, FAED 1, 166-67.

[*Et sint minores*];"[20] when this passage was read, he suddenly declared: "I wish that this brotherhood be called the Order of lesser brothers [*ut Ordo fratrum minorum fraternitas haec vocetur*]". And in fact, they were lesser – they who, being subject to all, sought always the lowest place and the most contemptible tasks in which they could meet with some affront.[21]

This narrative gives an account, not without convenient shortcuts, of a decisive institutional evolution: the passage – which here, under the stroke of inspiration, seems immediate – from the fraternity – and this, by the way, is the only occurrence of *fraternitas* in the entire *corpus* of the legends[22] – to the Order. It is a passage, if the legend which refers to the older of the two preserved versions of the *Rule* – the *Earlier Rule* – is to be believed, which would therefore be previous to the most recent draft, dated in 1223.

Pontifical sources confirm this evolution and allow us to know more exactly when it occurred. In the *Cum dilecti* of June 11, 1219, Pope Honorius III (1216–1227) presents Francis and his companions only as being part of "the life and the religion of the lesser brothers [*de vita et religione minorum fratrum*];" one year later, however, in the *Pro dilectis* of May 29, 1220, the same pontiff, without mentioning Francis, speaks thereafter of "the Order of

---

[20] ER 7:2: *Sed sint minores*.

[21] 1C 38. For the Latin text of the legends, *Fontes franciscani*, ed. E. Menestò and S. Brufani, Assisi (Testi, 2), 1995. English translation in *Francis of Assisi: Early Documents,* ed. R.J. Armstrong, J.A.W. Hellmann, W.J. Short, Vol. 1 (New York: New City Press, 1999), 217-18. Presentation of the principal legends in J. Dalarun, *The Misadventure.*

[22] T. Desbonnets, *From Intuition to Institution: the Franciscans* (Chicago, 1988), 73-82.

Friars Minor [*de Ordine fratrum minorum*]."²³ The turning point is therefore the year 1220.²⁴

This same shift was felt by the external observer Jacques de Vitry, that most extraordinary eyewitness of the times. Curate of Argenteuil perhaps even before being a priest, captivated by the Beguine Mary of Oignies, he would have been ordained in Paris around 1210; he finished by making his religious profession as a canon regular of St. Nicholas of Oignies, in the diocese of Liège. As a gifted orator he participates in preaching the crusade against the Albigensians, and follows this by preaching for the Fifth Crusade. In 1216, he is named Bishop of St. John of Acre, in the Holy Land, and composes the *Life of Mary of Oignies*, who had died three years earlier. He thus divides his time between the East and the West, from which experience he writes comparative histories. After relinquishing the episcopate of St. John of Acre, he becomes Cardinal-Archbishop of Tusculum in 1229. He dies in 1240, at the end of a life thoroughly dedicated to the service of the Church and to the struggle against heresy. His was an existence which united the East, the West, and Northern Europe with the diocese of Liège, and the South with the Italian Peninsula – the heart of the Curia and popular devotion. He lived in a state of constantly awakened curiosity, always on the alert for anything new, heedless of the blame or praise of others. In a letter composed in early October 1216, he introduces the new movement of the "lesser brothers" [*fratres minores*]" and the "lesser sisters [*sorores minores*],"

---

²³ W.R. Thomson, "Checklist of Papal Letters relating to the Three Orders of St. Francis. – Innocent III-Alexander IV," *Archivum franciscanum historicum*, 64, 1971, 367-580.

²⁴ R. Rusconi, "*Clerici secundum alios clericos*. Francesco d'Assisi e l'istituzione ecclesiastica," in *Frate Francesco d'Assisi. Atti del XXI convegno internazionale, Assisi, 14-16 ottobre 1993* (Spoleto, 1994), 71-100.

as a "religion [*religio*]."[25] Yet in a later missive, written in the spring of 1220, while he speaks again of the "religion of the lesser brothers, (*religio fratrum minorum*)," he refers also to their master "who instituted this Order (*Ordinem*)."[26]

There is most certainly an obvious and datable institutionalization, but it occurs in an Order that remains an Order of lesser brothers (*minores*). The social connotation of the very term *minores* has been pondered. Attilio Bartoli Langeli has carefully reread the charter of November 9, 1210 that marks the reconciliation between the *maiores* and *minores* in the political life of Assisi.[27] Since 1198, conflict had been breaking out between "the men of property (*boni homines*)" and "the men of the people (*homines populi*)." On one side was the aristocracy of knights, some of whom owned castles in the countryside, who lived together in the city below the Rocca in the exclusive cathedral quarter, traditionally loyal to the Empire and who had monopolized the local political offices during the commune's consular regime. The family of Clare of Assisi is part of this small circle of "princely" aristocrats. On the other side were the more recently established families who could not boast of knightly titles; these were the families called "popular" who were however definitely not of the "proletariat." To this group most certainly belongs the father of Francis, the wealthy and independent cloth merchant, Pietro di Bernardone. Was there a vague remembrance of "class consciousness" on Francis's part in the choice of the

---

[25] *Lettres de Jacques de Vitry (1160/1170-1240) évêque de Saint-Jean-d'Acre*, ed. R.B.C. Huygens (Leyde, 1960), 75-76.

[26] Id., *ibid.*, 131-132.

[27] A. Bartoli Langeli, "La realtà sociale assisana e il patto del 1210," in *Assisi al tempo di san Francesco. Atti del V convegno internazionale, Assisi, 13-16 ottobre 1977* (Assisi, 1978), 271-336.

term "lesser" or "minor" to identify his brothers? Attilio Bartoli Langeli conservatively sees this as coincidence.

We must come over to his opinion, for two major reasons. On one hand, from the end of the twelfth to the beginning of the thirteenth century, there were other religious groups who defined themselves as "lesser."[28] However, all of these did not have in mind the charter of 1210, or the balance between the socio-political and religious meanings of the term that Francis seems to have adopted in the particular case of Assisi. In another respect, the "lesser" model advocated by the Poverello in his very first fraternity was in no way that of an urban "bourgeois" religious life, but a joining in the conditions of the most powerless, who can be identified through the concrete study of their living conditions – for example, the seasonal agricultural worker[29] – in a movement that Giovanni Miccoli clarifies in these words:

> In Francis' eyes, a genuine Gospel way of life could be built only on such a choice [the choice of social arena]. As a result, the friars were able to unite two different life-styles, the religious life and the life of real poverty, a union which turned out to be substantially different from the traditions of religious life and thought that has developed over the centuries. This new way of Gospel life demanded that the friars practice true poverty and experience in their own lives what it really meant to be poor in Italian society in 1220.[30]

---

[28] G.M. Varanini, "Per la storia dei Minori a Verona nel Duecento," in *Minoritismo e centri veneti del Duecento*, dir. G. Cracco, Trente (Studi e testi, 7), 1983, 92-126, had observed the presence in the city of groups like the *pauperes minores S. Gabrielis*, who probably had nothing in common with the *fratres minores*.

[29] J. Dalarun, "Les maisons des frères: matériaux et symbolique des premiers couvents franciscains," in *Le village médiéval et son environnement. Études offertes à Jean-Marie Pesez* (Paris, 1998), 75-95.

[30] G. Miccoli, "A Christian Experience," 125.

In other words, it is the religious meaning of the term *minor* that is important. Minority here has a social meaning as well, but it is one that describes such an impoverished state of being that the *minores* of Assisi are as protected from it as are the *maiores*.

The choice of the term "minister [*minister*]" to designate those who lead the community is original, even if it is not an entirely Franciscan innovation. We have already heard this completely evangelical term within Francis's writings and in the frequent repetition which links it with "servant [*servus*]," as being in close harmony with the declaration of minority:

> And let the ministers and servants [*ministri et servi*] remember what the Lord says: I did not come to be served but to serve.[31]

The legends put this idea in real-life situations. A very long and very bitter section of the *Second Life*, written by Thomas of Celano in 1246-1247, is devoted to the perfect minister, such as the founder would have imagined him to be.[32] The minister general's role is defined through the use of imagery, which really does seem to be from Francis, as follows:

> After prayer, he says, he shall publicly announce his availability to be picked apart by all [*ab omnibus depilandum*], to respond to all, and to provide meekly for the needs of all.[33]

---

[31] ER 4:6, citing Mt 20:28. Cf. also LR 10:6. The insistence on the minister as servant nevertheless seems stronger in ER than in LR.
[32] 2C 184 -188.
[33] 2C 185.

Finally the founder himself most thoroughly accomplishes this deprivation, this total stripping of self which was the core of his religious project, by relinquishing the exercise of the office of "superior" – one hardly dares use this word – of the Order founded by his efforts.[34] The *Legend of Perugia*, in which is preserved a small section of material communicated to the Minister General Crescentius of Jesi (1244-1247) in 1246, probably coming from Brother Leo, reports the resignation's occurrence in this way:

> The blessed Francis wished to be humble among his brothers, and to preserve an even greater humility. During a chapter held at St. Mary of the Portiuncula a few years after his conversion, he resigned from his position as superior [*officium prelationis*] before all the brothers by saying, "From this moment on, I am dead to you. Instead, here is Brother Peter Cattani to whom we – you and I – will all be obedient." At that, all the brothers began to groan loudly and to weep great quantities of tears. Then blessed Francis, bowing before Brother Peter, promised him reverence and obedience. From this moment and until his death, he was made subject [*subditus*], like one of the other brothers.[35]

Over time, Francis seems to become dispossessed of his very self. Such is the picture presented in the legends, a picture including the application of the lessons taught in the writings, yet also omitting the fact that one can only resign from a position that he has previously accepted. Likewise, it must be noted, for example in the

---

[34] M. Cusato, *La renonciation* ..., 123-170.
[35] LP 105.

citation from the *First Life*, that the choice of the name "lesser brothers," completely full of superlative humility, allows a very decisive evolution – that of the passage from fraternity to Order – to come off smoothly. Francis of Assisi's refusal of power – ostentatious and emphatic – is nevertheless accompanied by an acceptance of the institution, of which an account must be given, including within its paradoxes.

ACCEPTANCE OF THE INSTITUTION

If we follow the accepted chronologies, Francis of Assisi, born around 1181, would have experienced his personal conversion around 1206. His example would have been gradually followed by others, the first companions, whose conversions are described in the *First Life* based on the obvious model of the apostles' recruitment in the Gospel.[36] Around 1209-1210, this community of a dozen individuals would have been equipped with an embryonic institutional framework defining its form of life; on a journey of the penitents to Rome, the pope would have verbally recognized its validity.[37] Two sources, a legend and the *Testament* of the founder, offer complementary and particularly clarifying points of view on this evolution.

The *Anonymous of Perugia*, written around 1240-1241 by a certain Brother John, companion of Brother Giles, is – even more than a legend – the chronicle of the passage *From Intuition to Institution*, to go back to the indicative title of the work by Théophile Desbonnets. The first companions have already gathered and Francis, always following the evangelical model, comes to exhort

---

[36] 1C 23-25 and 31.
[37] 1C 32-33.

them to go into the world and to call all people to do penance.[38] This wandering and intriguing – indeed disturbing – band arouses confusion:

> Some would ask them, "Where are you from?" Others would inquire further, "To what Order do you belong?" To these they would simply respond, "We are penitents and we were born in the city of Assisi," for the brothers' religion did not yet have the name "Order" (*religio fratrum non nominabatur Ordo*)."[39]

The response of the companions shows that, despite their ambition of a universal apostolate, their experience at that time is very rooted in a local reality – in this city of Assisi from which they all originate – but that it also lies within a proven canonical context – that of the penitential life. Since late Antiquity, the individual status of a/the penitent had been a recognized option for men and women – according to clearly differentiated norms for each sex – who chose to turn their backs on the values of the world. The golden age of the penitent is the beginning of the thirteenth century, which sees various *Rules* erected for the communal penitential life.[40] The narrator's commentary indicates however that, as far as the companions of Francis were concerned, this private status was not yet part of a specific communitarian enterprise; the religion of the brothers, meaning their form of religious life, was not – not yet – an Order. The venture was then developing at the local level, like so many other initiatives of the same era, under the

---

[38] AP 18.

[39] AP 19.

[40] G. Casagrande, "Un Ordine per i laici. Penitenza e Penitenti nel Duecento," in *Francesco d'Assisi e il primo secolo di storia francescana*, 237-255.

canonical control of the local ordinary – in this case the Bishop of Assisi,[41] into whose hands the son of Pietro di Bernardone had naturally placed himself from the time of his conversion.[42]

Let us now listen to the testimony of the one who's most concerned, in his *Testament.* This text with autobiographical value was dictated by Francis in the last days or weeks of his life, in the autumn of 1226. It is the most widely known of the Franciscan writings in the medieval tradition, referred to in one hundred twenty-five manuscripts. However, its actual circulation must have been much more considerable, since, according to the very terms of the *Testament,* ministers and custodians were always to have it at their fingertips, like the *Rule,* and to read it together with the *Rule* during the chapters.[43]

> The Lord told me, Brother Francis, in this way [*Dominus ita dedit mihi*] to begin to do penance: to know that, when I was in sin, it was extremely bitter for me to see lepers. And the Lord himself led me among them and I showed mercy to them. And when I left them, what had seemed bitter was changed for me into sweetness of soul and body. After that, I waited only a short while, and I left the world. [...] And after the Lord had given me brothers, no one showed me what I had to do, but the Most High himself revealed to me that I was to live according to the form of the Holy Gospel. And I, myself, had it written simply and

---

[41] N. D'Acunto, "Il vescovo Guido oppure i vescovi Guido? Cronotassi episcopale assisana e fonti francescane," in *Mélanges de l'École française de Rome: Moyen Âge*, 108 (1996), 479-524.

[42] 1C 14-15.

[43] Test 36-37.

in few words and the Lord Pope confirmed it for me.[44]

Neither here, nor in the following section of this text which lays down his last wishes in "a remembrance, an admonition, an exhortation,"[45] does Francis mention the word "Order," preferring always to speak of "brotherhood." Yet the thicket of regimental reminders that follow the passages cited and the allusions to the hierarchy that exists among the brothers truly prove that the institutionalization of this very unique experience stems from this pontifical confirmation – received from a pontiff who is not named – however it is perceived in the mind of the man from Assisi on the eve of his death.

The relationship between Order and founder is certainly one of the points that most sharply divide Franciscan hagiographers. For the so-called *Legend of the Three Companions* for example, – which was perhaps, in fact, written in 1246 by only two Brothers, Rufino and Angelo – the perfection of the saint's life and his prophetic clairvoyance come to legitimate the existence and the development of the Order.[46] On the contrary, for Bonaventure, in his *Major Legend*, the splendor of the learned Order, such as the minister general contemplates it in the 1260s with the eyes of a University-of-Paris-educated cleric, confirms the solid foundations of the otherwise very strange and disturbing experience of this

---

[44] Test 1-3 and 14-15. Regarding the legitimacy of the break in the text as it is shown here: F. Accrocca, *Francesco e le sue immagini. Momenti della evoluzione della coscienza storica dei frati minori (secoli XIII-XVI)*, Padua (Centro studi antoniani, 27), 1997, 15-35; J. Dalarun, *Postfazione, ibid.*, 238-239.

[45] Test 34.

[46] J. Dalarun, *The Misadventure*, pp. 189-204; Id., *Postfazione*, 244-251.

uncultured penitent from Assisi.[47] For Brother Leo, who in the *Legend of Perugia* sounds the nostalgic and bitter note of a guardian of supposedly lost ideals, Francis is a permanent reproach to the established and compromised Order of the 1240s.[48] But no one questions whether the saint accepted the mission to which Providence called him and the challenge thrown at him to create a community from the influx of brothers, and then to endow this community with the status of a recognized Order.

The account Francis gives of his conversion – the bitter changed to sweet through the grace of the lepers – is an admirable piece. The very brief passage by which he justifies what must be called, for future purposes, the foundation of the Order is, if one looks closely, remarkably audacious in its apparent simplicity. "The Lord told me [*Dominus dedit mihi*]" is the linchpin of the *Testament*. Is it extreme humility – or pride – to believe oneself so endowed by God, as the chosen of Providence? In fact, a founder, no matter how humble he claims to be, can always be described, in modern lingo, as a dissatisfied double of a megalomaniac. We say "dissatisfied" because he does not find his niche within any of the organizations offered by the Church, and God knows that there was no lack of them in the early thirteenth century! We say "megalomaniac" because he believes that he can offer something better, more in keeping with the times, more true to the teachings of the Gospel, and more useful to the Church than anything that existed before him.

But let us put aside that which, in this anachronistic vocabulary, is obviously only in jest. Beyond the lexicon

---

[47] G. Miccoli, *Francesco d'Assisi. Realtà e memoria di un'esperienza cristiana* (Turin, 1991), 265-302; J. Dalarun, *The Misadventure*, 221-258.

[48] J. Dalarun, *The Misadventure*, 204-219; Id., *Postfazione*, 244-251.

employed, the remark is nevertheless not so far out of place, at least in this particular era. The question – of knowing why Francis thought it was a good idea to found a new Order – was asked in the thirteenth century, by those both inside and outside the Order in question. Beginning in 1224-1225, the *Chronicle* of the monastery of Lauterberg posed the question, as concerned the institution of the Preachers and the Minors:

> But what is the meaning of introducing a new movement of this kind, unless it is in some reprobation for the careless and idle life led by those who are established in the Orders upon which the Church, up until now, had based itself?[49]

The author of this text is a Premonstratensian, a member of that Order of canon regulars living under the Augustinian *Rule*, founded by Norbert of Xanten in 1121. The commentary which follows is full of contradictions: the chronicler's oversensitive attachment to the old Orders, whose representative he purports to be, even if his spiritual family is barely one hundred years old; a wounded awareness of their loss of favor; irritation at the presumptiveness of these newcomers, who really could not rival Augustine or Bernard in sanctity; and yet, a suspicion that the new forms of religious life did respond better to the needs of the time.

The same question is again confronted, from the opening lines, in *Determinations of Questions Concerning the Rule of the Friars Minor*, formerly attributed to Bonaventure and indeed dating from the early second half of the thirteenth century: "Why did St. Francis

---

[49] *Chronicon Montis Sereni*, ed. E. Ehrenfeuchter, in *Monumenta Germaniae historica* (Hanover: Scriptores, 23, 1874), 220.

institute a new *Rule*?" And, for emphasis, the author adds: "as if the earlier saints' institutes did not suffice." The answer – a diplomatic one – is that the old institutes were either entirely monastic, or eremitical, or focused on an active apostolate, while the man from Assisi wished to bring these three characteristics together into a single Order, presented thus as an achievement and a great improvement over all the earlier attempts.[50] Be that as it may, the author, obviously a Friar Minor, felt the need of such a justification.

Francis really opened the door to these perplexing issues. "No one showed me what I had to do." Really! Was there not a single worthwhile priest to be found in all the clergy? Was there no organization that could fulfill his vocation to a life of penance? Of course, the *Testament* does not explain how one could be sure of a project's Providential backing without being influenced by controversy, the judgments of others, or even by the Church itself – to whom he has continually vowed complete and total submission; yet, how is it possible to read the document without even asking these questions? Francis receives direction only from the Most High; he finds recourse only in the Gospel. This is a double affront – again certainly completely involuntary, but for that very reason even more significant – to both the ecclesial institution and to Tradition. Likewise, if the *Testament* is to be believed, a few words and a spirit of great simplicity are all that are required to establish a form of life. Yet, we must again ask: is it evidence of incredible pretentiousness, or of extraordinary naïveté, to desire the confirmation of such a muddled mess by the pope personally?

---

[50] *Determinationes quaestionum super Regulam fratrum minorum*, in Bonaventure, *Opera omnia*, 8 (Quaracchi, 1898), 338.

As is emphasized in opposite ways by the two testimonies that were just cited, not only did Francis have the difficulty of choosing among the profusion of earlier religious institutions, but he already had a canonical status – that of the penitent – and because of this, he was doubly dependent upon the local ordinary – on the one, moreover, into whose hands he had religiously placed himself, body and soul: the Bishop of Assisi.

The *Testament* mentions no word of a trip to Rome and, in addition, gives no name to "the Lord Pope" who confirmed the original form of life. The first account of the trip of Francis and his companions to the papal city appears thus in the *First Life*,[51] which implicitly presents itself here as the complement of the autobiographical account of the founder. Thomas of Celano clearly names the pontiff to whom the penitents of Assisi submitted themselves: Innocent III (1198–1216), but he doesn't specify the date of the journey. Traditionally, the date has been fixed in 1209-1210, based on very uncertain evidence.

Usually, the testimony of the *Chronicle* of Burchard of Ursperg (d. 1230) is invoked. Under the year 1212, this author, in a jumbled fashion, in fact relates events dating from 1210 (the meeting of Bernard Prim and the Poor Ones reconciled with Innocent III in Rome, presented in reverse order, since the pope here seems to condemn what he had in reality approved)[52] and from 1216-1217 (the confirmation of the Order of Friars Preachers). Alongside these, he mentions the approbation of the *pauperes minores* by Innocent III, without a date and without the

---

[51] 1C 32-33.
[52] J. Sayers, *Innocent III: Leader of Europe 1198-1216* (London-New York, 1994), 148-50.

least allusion to a meeting in Rome.[53] Only the *First Life* and the *Anonymous of Perugia*,[54] among the early sources, give testimony to such a journey to the papal city during the time of Innocent III. The presence of Cardinal John of St. Paul in the stories places the episode before his death, in 1216. We must rely on the providential mention of Otto IV's (1198–1218) travel through Assisi, related some time later by Thomas of Celano – but with a date that is not at all certain, since it could be any time between 1209 and 1210 – in order to place the journey to Rome in this time frame. This is on the condition, however, that the hagiographer will have followed precisely the chronology of events, and not have inserted here the appearance of the emperor to fit his purposes.[55]

As if by chance, continues Thomas of Celano in his tale of the Roman rendezvous,[56] Guido, the Bishop of Assisi, finds himself also in the city at that time. At first very upset in his unexpected discovery of this step taken by the penitents, later, as the hagiographer tells us, he rallies to their cause. How can we believe this fortuitous encounter? What is more likely, which Thomas cannot mention, is that the Bishop of Assisi tried until the last minute – up to the pope's very doorstep in a kind of last-ditch effort – to block the request for official recognition and special protection from the Apostolic See that Francis had expressed in taking this very step. The prelate had clearly understood that such recognition would create universal acceptance of a movement that could have been the exclusive glory of his diocese. He also saw that such protection would lead, sooner or later, to an

---

[53] Burchard d'Ursperg, *Chronicon*, ed. O. Abel and L. Weiland, in *Monumenta Germaniae historica* (Hanover: Scriptores, 23), 1874), 376.

[54] AP 31-36.

[55] 1C 43.

[56] 1C 32.

exemption that would remove the penitents of Assisi from his episcopal control.

It serves no purpose to reflect on Francis of Assisi's pride,[57] since his psychological profile is not important in itself. The provocation such a profile would arouse could put the traditional view of Francis's institutional boldness as the height of humility – consistently presented by the saint, his hagiographers and all the later historians – in jeopardy. True perfection, for the Poverello, would have been to act as servant to the lepers who had brought about his conversion, in order to quickly share in their lot – one that was enviable because of its pain – which would have sent him, covered with sores, very quickly to the glory of the Father. Such was the clear direction given by Providence. This is not some wild and imaginary moralization; it is Francis himself who says it at the end of his life, according to the *First Life*:

> He wished again to go back to serving the lepers and to be held in contempt, as he was in the beginning. He considered leaving the company of others and moving to the most remote area possible, so that, free from all care and released from all preoccupation with others, he would no longer have anything but the provisional barrier of the flesh between God and himself.[58]

Yet, he did not do this. The care, the "preoccupation with others," weighed upon the founder until his dying breath; in this way, he maintained control.

Even though it obsessed a scholar like Paul Sabatier,[59] the Protestant minister, for reasons more subjective than

---

[57] J. Dalarun, *The Misadventure*, 217-19.
[58] 1C 103.
[59] P. Sabatier, *Vie de s. François d'Assise* (Paris, 1894).

objective,[60] and was likewise taken up in a very special way by Italian historians whose relationship with the Roman Church is never a neutral one, the question of the relationship with Rome is not the most important one. It is instead the contradiction between the refusal of power and the choice of institutionalization that is at the heart of what some writers have called – a little romantically – "the drama of Francis of Assisi." This is a drama whose existence the legends of the saint do not deny, but for which they – together with the great majority of later historians – offer the imprint of the stigmata as the reward for the sublimation of Francis's natural tendency to control. For our reflection, however, this contradiction in motives at the heart of the Franciscan experience is a godsend, for it requires everyone – Francis, his followers, and his hagiographers – to deny all responsibility for the institutional decision, to take apart its fundamental processes, and to put forward a kind of "bare bones" institution which allows it to be understood in its most basic essence.

The passage from the *Testament* cited previously is perfectly explicit in this regard: the institution, according to Francis, is first of all the adaptation of an individual's experience to a group endeavor – the passage from the *ego* to the *nos*. It is next the sowing of an idea, a vocation, and a mission in the social or geographic milieu, and in time. Through recognition by a superior authority, in this case the Apostolic See, an institution, the long-term existence of the idea, is guaranteed; it is transformed from the transitory into the permanent. The wrenching Franciscan issue is the keen awareness that, by being

---

[60] L. Pellegrini, "La 'Vie de saint François d'Assise' e gli studi francescani tra impegno critico e tensione ideologica," in *Francesco d'Assisi attesa dell'ecumenismo. Paul Sabatier e la sua "Vita di s. Francesco" cent'anni dopo* (= *Studi ecumenici*, 12), 1994, 11-30.

transformed into permanence, the transitory loses the qualities of the transitory. This perspective explains all the efforts at legislation by the Friars Minor and all the hagiographers' work of illustration. The institution guarantees existence. But what are the guarantees against the guarantee?

In this tense situation, three areas prove to be especially sensitive: the recruitment of brothers, the form of life which regulates their relationships, and the hierarchy that is established among them. Or, to leave it on the level of principle: who governs whom? And in what spirit?

PRINCIPLES OF GOVERNMENT

Once again we take up the journey to Rome, which represents all the key questions that interest us. The *Anonymous of Perugia* relates the departure of the young community in this way:

> Now, seeing that the grace of the Savior was increasing his brothers in number and in merit, blessed Francis said to them, "I see, brothers, that the Lord wishes to make of us a large congregation [*magnam congregationem*]. Let us therefore go to our mother the Roman Church; let us notify the Sovereign Pontiff what God is doing through us and that we will continue what we have begun according to his will and direction." And, because what he had said was agreeable to them, he took with him the twelve brothers and they went to Rome. And as they were setting out, he said to them: "Let us make one of us our leader [*ducem nostrum*] and let him be as the vicar of Jesus Christ for us [*vicarium Iesu Christi*]; wherever he desires

to go, we will go, and whenever he wants to stop, we will do it." And they elected [*elegerunt*] Brother Bernard, who had been received first by blessed Francis, and they did just as he had said.[61]

One can legitimately feel some reservation regarding the historicity of this account, which embroiders upon the *Testament*[62] and the *First Life*.[63] Yet the concern of the hagiographer-chronicler is clear: Providence has brought about a first rapid growth of companions around Francis, which foreshadows the influx of brothers to come; the dozen shaggy-haired penitents already see themselves as a "large congregation!" Duly noted. It is absolutely necessary to put this spontaneous community under the shelter of the Roman Church – and here is seen the part that is perhaps being played by the desire to cut short any suspicion of eccentricity or heresy. What is best: the group must be brought within the confines of the Church, the occasion of which becomes, in the tradition of the relationship between bishops and the Apostolic See, a veritable journey *ad limina apostolorum*.

There is a second piece of evidence – implicit this time, but which each of the later *Commentaries* of the *Rule* expands upon more than the last: every group of humans needs a leader. The choice of Bernard of Quintavalle, the "first born" of the companions, is an advance guarantee of continuity between the original fraternity and the Order to come. He is elected. There could be some discussion of the meaning of *eligere*: should "to elect" be understood in the sense most commonly used today, or more vaguely as "to choose"? Is Bernard designated like Matthias, the replacement for

---

[61] AP 31.
[62] Test 15.
[63] 1C 32.

Judas among the apostles, who had been chosen by lot, according to ancient democratic practices as well as to allow the divine will to be expressed?[64] Or is it instead done by a vote – a ballot – as is done for the Roman pontiff himself? This possibility indeed merits a closer look; the title proposed by Francis for this guide, "vicar of Jesus Christ [*vicarius Iesu Christi*]," is none other than the title assumed in this era by the successor of Peter.[65] In his own way, the hagiographer – obviously in a subdued way and with variations – replays the scene from the *Acts of the Apostles*. The Franciscan experience becomes a repetition, on another scale, of Church history, each one justifying the other, as Bonaventure afterwards will not hesitate to emphasize strongly.[66]

Yet to speak of the twelve, talking about them in this way, and to leave to the originator of the venture the role of the thirteenth – doesn't this prepare the way for a Poverello to become "another Christ [*alter Christus*]?"[67] The so-called *Legend of the Three Companions*, written in 1246 and which embroiders in its turn upon the *Anonymous of Perugia*, understood this tendency and its dangers so well, that, as a correction to its model, it felt the duty to make it clear, when introducing this same speech of Francis:

He, being the twelfth, their leader [*dux*] and their father, said to the eleven.[68]

---

[64] Acts 1:26.

[65] M. Maccarrone, *"Vicarius Christi." Storia del titolo papale* (Rome, 1952).

[66] Bonaventure, *Epistola de tribus quaestionibus ad magistrum innominatum*, in *Opera omnia*, 8 Quaracchi, 336.

[67] Acts 6:1

[68] L3C 46.

Nothing, however, will be able to prevent the eventual identification of the saint of Assisi with his Lord, an aspect so important that it would have to reappear sooner or later.[69] And the prudent aside from the *Legend of Three Companions* only raises another problem, without the author even suspecting its premonitory seriousness at this point in the tale: if the small community already had a spontaneous and providential guide, what will become of this person when another guide – *dux*, in both cases – is designated, elected, by human means?

In any case, in this presentation of the institution's reinvention, the hagiographers find it important to emphasize that the group that advances towards Rome, whatever its numerical size, is no longer a disorganized band, but that it is already, even at this embryonic stage, a living and breathing organism, whose life, however wandering it is, shall henceforth follow a definite and fixed pattern.

As regards the form of life submitted to Innocent III, no specific record of it has been kept. What is certain is that the rule-making effort continuously occupied – indeed obsessed – Francis from 1210 to 1226.

The *Earlier Rule*, in the form that has come down to us, is the result of a slow collection and ordering of precepts,[70] which begins under the pontificate of Innocent III (1198–1216) and is completed at the 1221

---

[69] The driving force behind this identification is expressed in Adm 5:1. J. Dalarun, *Postfazione*, 241.

[70] D. Flood, "The Genesis of the Rule," in D. Flood and T. Matura, *The Birth of a Movement: A Study of the First Rule of St. Francis* (Chicago, 1975), 3-56; G. Miccoli, *Gli scritti di Francesco*, 39-42; F. Accrocca, "Francesco e la sua Fraternitas. Caratteri e sviluppi del primo movimento francescano," in F. Accrocca and A. Ciceri, *Francesco e i suoi frati. La Regola non bollata: una regola in cammino*, Milan (Tau, 6), 1998, 9-124; A. Ciceri, "La Regula non bullata. Saggio storico-critico e analisi testuale," *ibid.*, 125-264.

Pentecost chapter.[71] The *Earlier Rule* – in Latin the *Regula non bullata* – is called this, because, despite the initial claim that the "Lord Pope," Innocent [III], had agreed to and confirmed this "life of the Gospel of Jesus Christ" for Francis and his brothers,[72] no letter ever arrived from the Papal Curia officially approving these legislative measures. Although it was soon obsolete, the *Earlier Rule* was nevertheless preserved in twenty-four manuscript copies of Franciscan writings, all of which belong to the so-called "Portiuncula" collection. In all respects, it has archeological value.

The *Later Rule*, on the other hand, was officially confirmed by the *Solet annuere* of Honorius III (1216–1227), which was issued from the Lateran on November 29, 1223. It is, moreover, in the original dispatch of the papal letter – in which is inserted the text of the *Rule* – and which is kept today in the Sacro Convento of Assisi, that the first manuscript copy of the *Rule* is to be found. Present in three out of four of the large collections of Franciscan writings and in ninety-six manuscript copies, this reference document was available in all the friaries of the Order as well.

Before even entering into the content of the regulations, before even attempting to determine which parts came from Francis personally and which came from

---

[71] This is different from the "Chapter of Mats" of which we will speak shortly, according to G. Miccoli, *La storia religiosa*, in *Storia d'Italia*, dir. R. Romano and C. Vivanti, II. *Dalla caduta dell'Impero romano al secolo XVIII*, 1 (Turin, 1974), 747-752.

[72] ER 2-3. This is also indicated in the first lines of the *Solet annuere* of Honorius III in 1223: "the *Rule* of your Order, approved by Pope Innocent, our predecessor of happy memory." On the relationship between the terms "Rule" and "Life": A. Tabarroni, "La regola francescana tra autenticità ed autenticazione," in *Dalla "sequela Christi" di Francesco d'Assisi all'apologia della povertà. Atti del XVIII convegno internazionale, Assisi, 18-20 ottobre 1990* (Spoleto, 1991), 81-85.

the intervention of others in the succession of revisions, a simple fact must be emphasized: the composition of a new *Rule* for a new Order could never be done by a single person. Writing rules and laws for the Friars Minor is a very demanding effort. It is also a challenge to Canon 13 of the Fourth Lateran Council, which had met in Rome in November of 1215 under the authority of Innocent III:

> For fear that excessive diversity of religious orders would cause serious confusion in the Church of God, we strongly forbid anyone henceforth to create a new order. Those who wish to enter religious life must choose from among those that are already approved. Likewise, those who wish to found a new religious order must assume a *Rule* and an institution from among the approved orders.[73]

These lines give an idea of what is at stake and what is represented in the recalling of a direct encounter of Francis and the Sovereign Pontiff before the council which enacted the fateful canon.[74] At the same time the hagiographers' insistence on the journey from Assisi to Rome becomes clearer. For, to slide into the reassuring mold of existing *Rules* is exactly what the founder will

---

[73] C.-J. Hefele, *Histoire des conciles d'après les documents originaux*, V, 2 (Paris, 1913), 1344.

[74] In the origin of multiple eremitic communities, which, by the *Licet Ecclesie catholice* issued by Alexander IV on April 9, 1256, comprise the Order of Hermits of Saint Augustine, the dictate of 1215 is omnipresent; F. Dal Pino, "Formazione degli Eremiti di sant'Agostino e loro insediamenti nella Terraferma veneta e a Venezia," in *Gli Agostiniani a Venezia e la chiesa di S. Stefano. Atti della giornata di studio nel V centenario della dedicazione della chiesa di Santo Stefano, Venezia, 10 novembre 1995* (Venice, 1997), 27-85.

not hear of, as is shown by this passage from the *Legend of Perugia*:

> On one occasion, blessed Francis found himself at the general chapter [*in capitulo generali*] near St. Mary of the Portiuncula – the one called the "Chapter of Mats" – which was attended by five thousand brothers, many of whom were wise and learned men. These went in search of the Lord Cardinal, the future Pope Gregory [IX], who was present at the chapter, and asked him to persuade blessed Francis to follow the advice of the so-called learned brothers, and to allow himself sometimes to be led [*interdum duci*] by them. They referred to the *Rules* of blessed Benedict, Augustine and Bernard, which teach their followers to live properly, according to this or that regulation. When he had listened to the cardinal's admonition on this subject, blessed Francis took him by the hand and brought him in front of the brothers assembled in chapter and he spoke to the brothers in these words: "My brothers, my brothers, God has called me to walk in the way of humility and has showed me the way of simplicity. I do not wish to hear you speak to me of any other *Rule* – not of Saint Augustine, nor of Saint Bernard, nor of Saint Benedict. The Lord told me that he wished for *me* to be a new fool in the world [*unus novellus pazzus in mundo*], and God did not wish to direct us by any other means than by this particular knowledge. But God will use your own knowledge and wisdom to confuse you. But as for me, I trust in the Lord's police [*castaldis Domini*] to punish you; then will you return in shame to your first state, whether you like it our not!" The cardinal, dumbfounded,

did not say a word and all the brothers were seized with fear.[75]

This is understandable; the outburst they have just been subjected to is a terrifying one, including even the calling up of the "Lord's police" which, in the founder's mind, are none other than demons. It is tempting, in this passage, to blame the attacks against knowledge on the hagiographer, in the much later context of the recording of the companions' remembrances in the 1240s, which is also the most significant era of the rapid expansion of the mendicants' *studia* and of the marginalization of the first companions themselves. However, the core of the argument must probably be brought back to Francis. The *Rules* that he rejects are the very ones implicitly advocated by the Fourth Lateran Council. This shows an independence of mind and a strong determination to follow the most difficult path, certainly. Doesn't the one who claims to be moved by inspired folly as opposed to the cold reason of men always appear in a better light? Yet this passage may be read another way: once again, humility and simplicity are placed in the service of a dictate. This is a very long way from the fraternal dialogue and group reflection that one could naively imagine to be specially favored in the chapter setting.

"And the Lord told me that he wished for *me* [*ego*] to be a new fool in the world." As in the *Testament*, the imperious claim of a direct connection with God proves the founder right in his folly. *Unus novellus pazzus in mundo.* The expression is *a priori* that of one who rebels against all authority. In fact, it is an attempt to establish

---

[75] LP 114. R. Brooke, *Early Franciscan Government. Elias to Bonaventura* (Cambridge, 1959), 286-291, and J. Moorman, *A History of the Franciscan Order from its Origins to the Year 1517* (Oxford, 1968), 54-55 agree at the placement of this Chapter "of Mats" at Pentecost of 1222.

his authority as absolute, without any discussion whatsoever. In this rejection of authority lies an abuse of power; in this explosion of the *ego*, there is prepotency, flung in the face of wisdom and knowledge. *Unus* when used as an article is a vulgarism of the first order. *Pazzus* is the reflection of the Pauline *stultus*.[76] But, again, the Italian turn of the phrase guarantees the authenticity of Francis's *logion*, as does the diminutive *novellus,* which one has rambled on so much about and which must certainly be seen, together with the reference to the Pauline folly, as a reference to the advent of the New Covenant.[77] There is nothing like laying claim to such a folly for sending the wisdom of the sages to the devil.

What, then, is the project that justifies such a fury? We will have to return to the precise way the two principal preserved *Rules* function. The *Earlier Rule,* as we have seen, mixes together multiple successive stages, and Caesar of Speyer, a well-educated brother who joined the Order in 1219 or 1220, intervenes to insert the appropriate biblical citations into the document. The *Later Rule* was the object of a thorough re-writing, in which the future Gregory IX – then Cardinal Hugolino – boasts to have played an important part. The lesser-known text of the *Rule for Hermitages* seems on the other hand to supply the component which is not original, for it is possible that it was composed after the *Later Rule,* but which is primary to the conception of community, community life, and government according to Francis of Assisi. While this document certainly was put into practice in only a limited way, its presence in three of the large collections of manuscripts and in twenty-two copies of Franciscan writings guarantees its authenticity.

---

[76] 1 Cor 4:10. G. Miccoli, *Il Testamento di san Francesco,* Magnano, 1984; *Le Testament de saint François* (Paris, 1996), 78-79.

[77] J. Dalarun, *Francis of Assisi and the Feminine,* 273-74.

For those who wish to remain in a religious manner
in hermitages: let them be three or at most four
brothers. Let two of them act as mothers who
have two, or at least one, as (a) son(s). Let the two
who are the mothers lead the life of Martha and
the two sons lead the life of Mary. [...] However,
from time to time, let the sons in their turn take
on the role of the mothers, for as long as it seems
good to them to do so.[78]

The newness of this very experimental text can
only be understood in relation to the long history of
monasticism.[79] The great reforms of the eleventh and
twelfth centuries, such as had occurred at Cluny, for
example, had introduced a fundamental break with
traditional Benedictine monachism. Almost all the Orders
created after the Year 1000 are actually double Orders;
they are not necessarily mixed, but double – made up
of two parts. While the lay servants of Cluny's domain
were forbidden religious status and all other association
with their masters' project except that of producing, by
the sweat of their brow, the sustenance which supported
these aristocratic monks in their long hours of prayer, the
Order of Citeaux, founded in 1098 by Robert of Molesme,
grants a place to the "ignoble" segment of society. The
lay brothers live alongside the choir monks. The former
are simple lay people, but they nevertheless wear the
religious habit; the latter, being from a higher social
class – sons of knights, and educated – are priests. Thus

---

[78] RH 1-2 and 10.

[79] *Les religieuses dans le cloître et dans le monde. Actes du 2ᵉ colloque
international du C.E.R.C.O.R., Poitiers, 19 septembre-2 octobre 1988*
(Saint-Étienne, 1994); *Les mouvances laïques des Ordres religieux. Actes
du troisième colloque international du C.E.R.C.O.R., en collaboration
avec le Centre international d'études romanes, Tournus, 17-20 juin 1992*
(Saint-Étienne, 1996).

is created a double Order, just like the Congregation of Vallombreuse, an Order founded earlier in the first half of the eleventh century by John Gualbert (d. 1073) and which saw the birth of this great innovation of the lay brother.

Another double religious institute was the one attempted by Stephen of Muret (d. 1124), which moves to Grandmont after the founder's death. Here the lay brothers coexist with the priests, as at Citeaux, but they are one and all engaged in a project that is infinitely more daring: it is the lay brothers, as "Marthas," who govern the priests, the "Marys." Dominic, in Francis's time, wished to establish the same principle in the Order of Friars Preacher, by entrusting the government of the community to the lay brothers. The failure of Grandmont served to dissuade him from this plan. In the double – and in this case, mixed – Order of Fontevrault, founded in 1101 by Robert of Arbrissel, there is an additional development: in a revolution seen as contrary to the natural order, it is the women who are in charge of the men. Actually, Fontevrault is much more than double: the religious men are divided into priests and lay people, while the nuns are separated into virgins and celibates. Here – very scandalous indeed – it is the celibate nuns, the "Marthas," who are in charge and the "Marys" and the "Johns" who assist them. Another four-part Order, the Order of Sempringham, attempted by Gilbert (d. 1189), consists of the men, as priests and lay brothers, and the women, as virgins and celibates, all under the authority of a single ruler.

These combinations of increasing – it would be tempting to say more and more torturous – complexity form a chronological frame around the Reform of the Church and of Christianity known as "Gregorian," after Gregory VII (1073–1085); they answer the aspiration – to counter the Empire's ambitions to rule the world and the ecclesial system – that each and every person be directly concerned with the salvation of humanity, which would henceforth be experienced as a community of individuals needing salvation. They are the products and the continuation of a discovery of the Gospel that is at the same time both deeper and wider in scope.

They correspond also to a society – that of the turning of the eleventh and twelfth centuries – that is most certainly bitter and inflexible in its internal divisions, but in which the arrival of new sources of wealth, the rebirth of cities, the rapid growth of schools, and the increase in monetary circulation give rise to forms of distinction that are simultaneously more fluid and more subtly marked. The religious founders, as inspired experimenters, indeed endeavor to express schematically and symbolically their conception of society – as a two-part structure which could perhaps be broken into four parts – through the use of antinomical pairings which represent the whole world, all of society, and all of Christianity. These could be translated, in today's language, as: all social classes, all states of life, and, also, both sexes.

Division and intermingling within Orders by state of life or sex, at Fontevrault or at Sempringham, create a four-part world within the cloister in order to signify emblematically that the entire world is called to salvation, that everyone is called to work actively with others for his own salvation as for humanity's. To ensure a clear conscience, to make progress in the struggle against worldly powers, to transpose clashes of power into the realm of belief and of individual responsibility: such was indeed the response – and what a bold response it turned out to be! – given by the Church to the Empire and to the princes.

One century later, the new Franciscan movement joins in the continuous progression of this plural movement, but it also pushes this movement to its limit.

In the *Rule for Hermitages*, which utilizes role-playing, the figures of Martha and Mary – the same categorization used by Fontevrault, Grandmont, and the Friars Preacher – correspond not to a pre-determined social rank, state of life, or sexual identity. Lazarus's two sisters serve only to express two functions, which are provisional – "from time to time [*quandoque*]" – and interchangeable – "in their turn [*vicissitudinaliter*]."

In the very early days of his fraternity, before the arrival of the structured novitiate with the *Cum secundum* of September 22, 1220[80] or the division between priests and brothers that began in 1239, and, most of all – in this Order of servants' servants! – before the great proliferation of secular servants,[81] Francis indeed tried to welcome anyone who asked into his penitential project, without distinguishing by level of birth, social status, education, and certainly even without distinguishing by sex.[82] This is still what is shown by the spirit of the *Rule for Hermitages*, as an outlying example of a "Franciscan Utopia"[83] in the process of being eroded by confrontation with reality. The religious project of the penitents of Assisi is to share in the life of the most marginalized, but

---

[80] A clause which seems to respond line for line to the reproaches expressed by Jacques de Vitry in the spring of 1220 regarding the "extremely dangerous religion [*religio valde periculosa*]," which sends young people into the world without formation; *Lettres de Jacques de Vitry...*, 131-132. This is the clause that LR 2 puts into practice.

[81] Numerous enough to be officially exempt from the interdict in 1248; Gratien de Paris, *Histoire de la fondation et de l'évolution de l'Ordre des frères mineurs au XIIIe siècle*, new ed. Mariano d'Alatri and S. Gieben, Rome (Bibliotheca seraphico-capuccina, 29), 1982, 189. In LP 10, it is obvious that, at St. Mary of the Portiuncula, the clerics of the Order are served by the brothers who are not priests and by lay servants.

[82] J. Dalarun, *Francis of Assisi and the Feminine*, 273-74.

[83] A. Vauchez, "François d'Assise," in *Au temps du renouveau évangélique, 1054-1274*, dir. A. Vauchez, Paris (Histoire des saints et de la sainteté chrétienne, 6), 1986, 149.

the true boldness of Francis lay in belief that the most marginalized can theoretically share on the same level in the life of the community.[84]

What an unheard of suggestion! Let us clearly understand: it is a suggestion that religious life can be inclusive of the most marginalized, without the all-embracing project that is attributed to a Romuald, the founder of the Camaldoli in 1010, to "change the entire world into the desert." There is no missionary fever with Francis, at least in the West. Witness is to be given by being who you are, more than by words; the rest is a matter of grace.[85]

In opening this door, the man from Assisi was responding also to the challenge to religious life to heal what Jacques Le Goff had called "a society in pieces, one that displays the remainders of varied but partial structurations."[86] Central Italian society – a small world, but one with a high degree of complexity in its social categories – reassured no one that the unity of Christianity could restore the basic and harmonious order of things. In Chapter 23 of the *Earlier Rule*, Francis has to compile a list of not less than forty categories in an attempt to express the totality of Christian society. His response, in the form of a religious proposition, such as it appears in the *Rule for Hermitages*, is the repetition of the *Epistle to the Galatians*:

---

[84] Such is the case, in LP 19, of Brother John the Simple, who comes from a small peasant village. This is a theoretical possibility, but certainly the exception in practice; on the social recruitment of the first companions: T. Desbonnets, *From Intuition to Institution*, 18-20.

[85] J. Dalarun, *Postfazione*, 242-43.

[86] J. Le Goff, *art. cit.*, 115.

There is neither Jew nor Greek, there is neither slave nor free person, there is not male and female, for you are all one in Christ Jesus.[87]

One cannot help but be struck, in the same way, by the uncommon nature of the passage in the *Admonitions* in which Francis tells the story of the Fall without the intervention of Eve,[88] as if Adam sufficed to represent all of humanity, including its feminine component, thus exonerating the feminine from its particular culpability that the story of Genesis had always laid heavily upon it. It is not anachronistic to say that there was in Francis of Assisi a unique perception of humanity.

Beyond the interchangeable nature of the functions, which implies an absence of *a priori* categorization of individuals, the *Rule for Hermitages* also conveys a new notion of government. Martha and Mary are the two sisters of Lazarus – the active and the contemplative.[89] At Fontevrault, these two Gospel figures were applied to two groups of women – celibates and virgins. In Stephen of Muret's and Dominic's Orders, the two sisters already come to represent the status and functions of two groups of men. For Francis, there is the same slide from the feminine to the masculine – the two women represent men – but it is accompanied by a slide between generations and, secondly, by a reversal of roles: the Marthas become mothers and the Marys, sons.

The ultimate goal of these evangelical-anthropological variations – what the Assisian is attempting to convey – is that the only mode of government reconcilable with the principle of absolute brotherhood is that of relative

---

[87] Gal 3:28.
[88] Adm 2. Cf. J. Dalarun, *Francis of Assisi and the Feminine*, 30-32 and 263-66.
[89] Lk 10:38-42.

motherhood. Moreover, the anthology of Francis's sexual contraventions has already been drawn up: he addresses Leo "as a mother [*sicut mater*];" he is called "dear mother" by Pacifico; he has a dream in which he is a black hen trying to gather her chicks under her wings; he describes himself as a poor woman of the desert impregnated by a king, and as a statue of a noble lady made of a metal alloy that brings to mind the dream of Nebuchadnezzar; he is hailed under the title of "Lady Poverty."[90]

"The abbot as mother" is not a new idea, as was proved by Carolyn W. Bynum.[91] It is found throughout monastic spirituality. To advocate maternal government is first of all a clever way not to contradict the Gospel, in the already cited verse from Matthew:

> As for you, do not be called "Rabbi." You have but one teacher, and you are all brothers. Call no one on earth your father; you have but one Father in heaven. Do not be called "Master;" you have but one master, the Messiah.[92]

To cast oneself as mother is also, paradoxically, to assert a new and perfect imitation of Christ, whose spiritual maternity was sung by the same ones who meditated on abbatial maternity, – in particular, those close to Citeaux. Here again, however, Francis rushes with particular force into what was, until he came, only one potentiality among others.

Proof of this power of expression is given by the *Canticle of the Creatures*. While this famous text did not gain an enormous medieval audience, as is shown

---

[90] J. Dalarun, *Francis of Assisi and the Feminine*, 30-32 and 263-66.

[91] C.W. Bynum, *Jesus as Mother. Studies in the Spirituality of the High Middle Ages* (Berkeley-Los Angeles-London, 1982).

[92] Mt 23:8-10.

by eleven manuscripts that belong to the only two large collections of Franciscan writings, the story of its composition is fully recounted in the *Legend of Perugia*.[93] The poem, unique in this genre among the Franciscan writings (along with *The Canticle of Exhortation for the Ladies of San Damiano*, whose authenticity is however always a matter of debate), is written in the language of the people – in the Umbrian dialect – and therefore in the mother tongue. Because of this, it is one of the very first monuments of Italian Literature. To sing the praise of the Creator through his creatures, Francis brought into his verse the two lights and the four elements, who, for each type, answer each other three by three. "Sir Brother Sun" is followed by "Sister Moon and the Stars." The alternation of masculine and feminine continues with "Brother Wind" – for the Italian *aria*, unlike the Latin *aer*, would end up disturbing the harmonious apportionment of grammatical categories – and "Sister Water," then "Brother Fire" and "our Sister Mother Earth." Here, Francis could not keep to the simple allocation between brothers and sisters; he felt the need to endow the earth – which is both a component of matter ("earth" with a small "e") and the nourishing environment where humanity lives ("Earth" with a capital "E") – with a double meaning which stretches the bond of kinship across two generations:

> Praised be you, my Lord, for our Sister Mother Earth
> who sustains and governs us
> and produces varied fruits
> with colored flowers and the grass.[94]

---

[93] LP 43, 44, 51 and 100.
[94] CtC 9.

Cristiana Garzena recently brought to light a point that had been overlooked until now.[95] Going back over the course of Ancient and Christian Tradition, in particular the succession of commentaries on *Genesis*, she showed that the idea of an earth that "governs" never appears in the earlier sources; ordinarily, it is the people who govern the earth. Here, the semantic ambiguity of the verb *governare* is certainly being played upon. The earth "governs" like she "sustains" us – a simple reduplication which indicates that she provides nourishment and shelter. Indeed, in Italian, one "governs" the children (in the sense that one takes care of them), the house, the horses, the grain (by removing the weeds), the eggs (by watching over them until they hatch), the fire (by feeding it), and the wine (by watching over the wine-making process). Nevertheless, the classical meaning of "to govern" (to be in charge of), which cannot be excluded, opens the possibility of a return to the traditional relationship between the earth and humankind: that which is governed (the earth) becomes the governess. However, isn't it true that, even today, all it takes is for the one who governs to change from male to female in style (as is the case with the traditionally female "earth,") for the role to become that of a servant?

At the time when he dictated this verse of the *Canticle of the Creatures* and chose to use the non-traditional sense of the word "to govern," Francis must have had in mind, at a level of consciousness impossible to determine, the question that required all of his energy in the last years of his life: the government of a religious Order – the government of the Order founded by his efforts. The dual nature of the government of the earth is the image of the ministry of the "minister:" governing, but as a

---

[95] C. Garzena, *Terra fidelis manet. Humilitas e servitium nel "Cantico di frate Sole,"* Florence (Saggi di "Lettere italiane," 50), 1997.

servant and not as a lord; superior, but like an inferior; *maior* because of being *minor* and *minor* because of being *maior*.

The refusal of domination in all its forms; acceptation of the institution, although kind of forced by the Providence; theoretical openness to a humankind without distinctions; a community that would only comprise functions, without any distinctive status; an alternative government of service expressed through the figure of the mother: such appear to be the principles – defended passionately by the founder even at the peril of having to renounce some of them – of a brotherhood that became an Order in 1220. What remains is to explore their concrete application, during the time of Francis and of his first successors.

CHAPTER TWO

MODES OF GOVERNMENT
IN THE ORDER OF FRIARS MINOR

How did the Friars Minor conceive of and practice the government of their Order? The first surprise is to note that this question, in the profusion of Franciscan studies, has hardly held the attention of historians, with the exception – as is usually the case when it concerns pioneering inquiries – of Giulia Barone.[1] A recent summary volume on *Francesco d'Assisi e il primo secolo di storia francescana* does not devote any specific study to it.[2] The point of view adopted in the pages that follow will be above all "constitutional" – regarding the source of power and the distribution of powers. In concrete terms, two indicators will be examined as a matter of priority – ministers and chapters, as well as, of course, the relationships between

---

[1] G. Barone, "Note sull'organizzazione amministrativa e la vita delle province nei primi decenni di storia francescana," in *Studi sul Medioevo cristiano offerti a Raffalelo Morghen per il 90° anniversario dell'Istituto storico italiano (1883-1973)*, Studi storici, 83-87 (Rome, 1974), 57-70. For a general overview, Gratien de Paris, *Histoire de la fondation* ... ; R. Brooke, *Early Franciscan Government* ... ; J. Moorman, *A History of the Franciscan Order*, pp. 1-304; G. Miccoli, *La storia religiosa*, 734-93; T. Desbonnets, *From Intuition to Institution*.

[2] See, however, the lucid synthesis in this volume by G.G. Merlo: "Storia di frate Francesco e dell'Ordine dei Minori," in *Francesco d'Assisi e il primo secolo di storia francescana*, 3-32.

them: designation and attributions of the former, and composition and precedence of the latter. After some points of comparison taken from the history of religious institutes, that which concerns the government of the Friars Minor will be clarified by reading, successively, from the Assisian's writings, from his legends, from the chronicles of the Order, and, finally, from the legislation produced after the founder's death.

A BASIS FOR COMPARISON

In an article published in 1958, "Note On the Evolution of Electoral Processes In Religious Orders From the Sixth to the Thirteenth Century",[3] Leo Moulin focuses his attention on the question of the procedures for selection of delegates and election to government in the Church.[4] The author clarifies:

Whether we like it or not, it is the electoral process, more than principles, which, in the last analysis, influences both the nature of the balloting and the nature of the governmental system itself. A publicly given unanimous vote is not at all the same as a majority vote arrived at by secret ballot. The first gives rise to dictatorial methods; the second is the most important requirement for every democratic system of government.[5]

---

[3] L. Moulin, "'Sanior et maior pars.' Note sur l'évolution des techniques électorales dans les Ordres religieux du VIe au XIIIe siècle," in *Revue historique de droit français et étranger*, 36 (1958): 368-97 and 491-529.

[4] The author has devoted numerous articles to the same subject. The article cited here seemed to offer a clear synthesis of his earlier works; likewise L. Moulin, *La vie quotidienne des religieux au Moyen Âge, Xe-XVe siècle* (Paris, 1978), 191-244.

[5] L. Moulin, "Sanior et maior pars," 369.

Leo Moulin then develops a portrait of the electoral processes within the Church, for pontiffs as well as for the leaders of religious Orders. The myth of unanimous election predominates until the eleventh century, but, in practice, cases of decisions made by the majority are found beginning with a papal election of the third century – that of Cornelius, in 251 – and in the deliberations of the Councils of the fourth and fifth centuries. The main impetus, however, is provided by the Benedictine *Rule* which, for the election of the Abbot, provides for the following of the counsel of "the soundest part [*senior pars*]" and, it clarifies, "no matter how small [*quamvis parva*]." It remains only to know who qualifies as the *senior pars* – a particularly insoluble problem in papal elections. Because of this, appearing at the Second Lateran Council in 1179 is the principle of papal election by a majority of two-thirds of those present, a principle which has not been changed since that time, which was spread to numerous religious institutes and in which Leo Moulin sees the origins of the current "qualified majority." Even in the twelfth century, *senior* regularly flanks *maior* for forming the "sounder and larger part [*senior et maior pars*]." It is perhaps at the Fourth Lateran Council, in 1215, where the determining weight of the *maior pars*, as a criterion distinct from the *senior,* is affirmed for the first time, by Canon 24. In any case, the principle of vote by absolute majority prevails in the Church in the thirteenth century, while the principle of secret ballot will be important in the sixteenth century.

This brief summary of an article, moreover, abounding in information, suffices to raise some confusing issues. First of all, it is not certain that an electoral process, as important as it may be, could be established as a sufficient criterion for a "democracy." Proof of this lies in the fact that the people of old thought of the random drawing as a completely democratic method of selection – as much as an election,[6] which, they considered, could even be subject to cheating. Within the aspect of the balloting lay the questions of the extent of the "electoral body," of the identity of the electorate, and when it's a question of "representative electors," of the method for their own selection and, consequently, of their possible representative character. It is not certain, moreover, that the process for choosing a person for a given office and the method for making a collective decision can be one and the same. Concerning the choice of a single individual for an office, there are certainly multiple influences between papal and episcopal elections, and between the selection of superiors of a religious Order, and one Order may certainly influence another. But this story does not develop in a linear fashion; these influences are not mechanical; innovations or delays are not innocently made. Each one of these evolutions, whether of a pioneering or backward nature, can only be understood in relation to each institute's identity, to its sensibility, its spirituality, and its own particular tradition.

To put these institutional or statutory choices back in context is both to escape the risk of a progressive linear vision of history and to avoid an obsession with origins – here the origins of the Modern Democracy, which would thus be "Christian Democracy" – a quest from which, as is seen, it is difficult to remove all ideological reasoning.[7]

---

[6] Aristotle, *Politics*, IV, 14-15.

[7] L. Moulin is nevertheless defined as an "agnostic political expert" by T. Desbonnets, *From Intuition to Institution*, 158.

Leo Moulin is perfectly right to emphasize how much the Fourth Lateran Council, beginning in 1215, becomes the reference and crucible for all reflection on the foundational procedures of institutional operation in the Church. We have already mentioned Canon 13, which forbade the invention of new forms of religious life.

Canons 23 through 26 dealt with the elections of pastors of Regular or Cathedral churches – or to put it plainly, bishops or superiors of monasteries. Canon 23 aims at preventing a position's vacancy from being longer than three months. If the chapter has not succeeded in determining the superior during this time frame, it loses its power in the matter. The responsibility for making the selection then goes to the next highest level of authority presiding at the church in question – again, in less than three months, with the advice of his own chapter. Canon 24 attempts to prevent a harmful diversity in electoral procedures. Three trustworthy persons, designated by the electorate, will gather the votes "in secret and one by one," put them down in writing, and announce the results. "Either the largest or the soundest part [*vel maior vel sanior pars*]" of the chapter will prevail; it is here, where, for the first time, according to Leo Moulin, *partes maior* and *sanior* are distinguished from one another – the first being emancipated from the second. But the "electoral power [*potestas eligendi*]" may still be entrusted to a few, who "on behalf of all [*vice omnium*]," will choose the pastor, unless – the last canonical possibility – the election is accomplished "as by divine inspiration." The proxy is accepted only in the event of an impediment. Canon 25 attempts to block the secular abuse of power in ecclesiastical elections. The next one reminds the reader that the "completeness of the office [*plenitudo officii*]" takes effect only after confirmation by the superior authority. The confirming authority must not only examine the person who is elected, but also the electoral procedure. For the offices reporting directly to the pope, it is appropriate to solicit confirmation by the same.[8]

The procedure is clear in its overall design and in a number of its details. The power to choose and to confirm, both necessary for a complete "election," are clearly distinguished from one another: the first a matter of concern for the collegial administration – direct or delegated, the second for the hierarchy. The foundation for the entire structure is the chapter, the same term being used for the elections of regular and secular pastors. On the other hand, not specified at all are the duration of the superior's duties and the position of the chapter members – "those who must and wish to and are readily able to participate."[9] The clause, in its imprecision, evidently respects the plurality of the institutional traditions.

The importance of chapters and the standardization of the way they were run is at the heart of Canon 12 of the Council of November 1215:

> In every kingdom or province shall be held, every three years, without ignoring the rights of the bishops, a common chapter of Abbots and of Priors for houses not possessing an Abbot, who are not in the custom of holding such chapters. Let all those not facing any canonical impediment go there, to one of the monasteries that are able to accommodate them.

---

[8] C.-J. Hefele, *Histoire des conciles* ... , 1352-1355.
[9] *Ibid.*, 1353.

Provision is made for two Cistercian Abbots from nearby to be present, to offer aid and counsel in virtue of their long experience in the convening of such chapters. Assisted by two other participants, they will preside over the assembly, allowing the Cistercian way of doing things to be seen. The reform and the regular observance of the *Rule* will be discussed. All that will be decided upon and approved by the four Presidents must be scrupulously respected. At the end of the meeting, the location of the next chapter will be determined. The visitators – those who will see to the correction of the men's and women's religious houses and who will report incompetent superiors to the Ordinary – will be designated. Bishops and chapter presidents will continue to guard against the abuses of the monasteries' lay dependents.[10]

The text of 1215, in its attempt to bring order to a disturbing diversity, straightforwardly sanctions the superiority of the Cistercian model over that of all other religious institutes. The operation of the abbeys dependent upon Citeaux was determined, in its overall design, from the time of the founding document constituted by the *Carta caritatis*, approved by Callistus II (1119–1124) in 1119 (*Carta caritatis prior* being attributed to Abbot Stephen Harding). It was clarified by brief statutes contained in the *Summa Cartae caritatis* dated 1123–1124, and revised from 1152 to 1165 (*Carta caritatis posterior*), after which the document remains unchanged.[11] This is not the place to recount the stratigraphy of this legislation. What interests us above all is an inevitable reference on the horizon of the experience of the Friars Minor. We know that the main aspects of the Cistercian

---

[10] C.-J. Hefele, *Histoire des conciles* ... , 1342-1343.

[11] *Les plus anciens textes de Cîteaux*, ed. by J. de la Croix Bouton and J.B. Van Damme, Achel (Cîteaux – Commentarii cistercienses – Studia et documenta, 2), 1985.

model, while respecting the absolute economic autonomy of each establishment, aimed to safeguard the unity of the group gathered around the abbey of Citeaux – the oldest texts pay only lip service to the terms "Order" or "congregation" – through the means of filiations of mother abbeys to daughter abbeys.

The Abbot of the founding monastery visits all his daughter abbeys annually. In 1163, Citeaux itself, which had been exempt from visits until then because it was the original mother monastery, became subject to this provision; it would be visited by the Abbots of the first four daughter houses: La Ferté, Pontigny, Clairvaux and Morimond.

The cohesion of the group of establishments thus spread abroad is assured by the "general chapter," which meets each year at Citeaux ("the new monastery [*novum monasterium*]," as opposed to Molesme). This chapter meets at a date decided upon mutually by common accord, and includes the Abbots of all the monasteries – and the monks of the abbey of Citeaux, according to an arrangement that vanishes in 1165 – under the presidency of the Abbot of Citeaux. Here, the salvation of souls is discussed; here, all the ways of respecting the observance of the *Rule* are determined; here, the lax Abbots are rebuked. In 1165, it is specified that, if an agreement were not reached during the deliberations, the Abbot of Citeaux and the wisest among them would settle the question. If he is unable to attend because of poor health, an Abbot may be replaced by his Prior. It is firmly prohibited for any abbey to hold chapters separately with its daughter abbeys. Clearly, the filiations must be channels of unity and in no way sources of any type of particularism.

The Abbot of Citeaux, with the aid of his Prior, admonishes the Abbots who are in the wrong. If the guilty party persists, the Abbot of his mother abbey brings it to the attention of the area bishop and to his chapter. If he still does not mend his ways, the Abbot of Citeaux and some other Abbots come into the monastery, depose the obstinate one and preside at the election of a successor by the monks of the establishment. If the abbey of Citeaux itself becomes lax, the Abbots of La Ferté, Pontigny and Clairvaux – and of Morimond, added in 1165 – will discipline its Abbot. If he persists, he is deposed and his successor is chosen by the monks of Citeaux, in the presence and with the counsel of the Abbots of the direct daughter-houses of Citeaux; in 1165, this is amended to: by the monks of Citeaux and by the Abbots of the direct daughter-houses. The Abbot of La Ferté certifies the vacancy. The procedure is the same in the event of the death of the Abbot of the founding monastery. For the other abbeys, the superior is elected by the monks of the place – plus the Abbots of the future daughter abbeys, as is added in 1165 – under the presidency of the Abbot of the mother abbey; the superior may be chosen from among the monks of the place, from Citeaux, or from any other monastery of the Order.

As we see, the system is based on a subtle equilibrium between the autonomy of each house and the cohesion of all. There are many measures for getting rid of bad superiors, but, on the other hand, this is tied to the fact that, in those days, their office was certainly held for life, and thus their power was considerable and at risk of being diverted. The monks, with the exception of course of the lay brothers, had real power at their disposal to choose superiors, and those from Citeaux had more than the others. But it is clear, especially after the modifications of the 1160s, that by their exclusive presence at the general chapter, their personal control over the daughter abbeys, their collective control of Citeaux, their dominating role in the election of its abbot, and their possible influence in the elections of the other superiors, the abbots formed a type of oligarchy within the Order which reserved a monopoly for itself on all vertical or horizontal relationships.

THROUGH THE FRANCISCAN WRITINGS

Let us return to the Order of Friars Minor and look again at its overall structure. Francis had accepted – around 1209 or 1210, let's say – that his brotherhood was becoming a religious institute, then, exactly in 1220, that his institute was making itself into an Order. The term, however, seems to be repugnant to him, even though the vast majority of his writings are after this fundamental date: as we've seen, he doesn't use it in the *Testament*; he uses it very rarely in the other texts, and his *Letter*, incorrectly known as *to the Entire Order*, which is present in the four large manuscript collections of Franciscan writings, attested to in fifty-three copies, and was composed at the very end of his life, is in fact addressed

> to the minister general of the *religion* of lesser brothers, its lord [here, meaning Brother Elias], and to the other minister generals who will come after him and to all the ministers and custodians and priests of this same *brotherhood*, humble in Christ, and to all its brothers, simple and obedient – to the first ones and to the most recent.[12]

---

[12] LtOrd 2. It isn't until LtOrd 38 that "to the priests of our Order" is found. There is also the following in TPJ 4: "all the masters of Paris have joined the Order," and the allusion in LR 7:2 to "the priests of the Order."

Nevertheless, Honorius III, as we've emphasized, does speak of the *Ordo* in the *Pro dilectis*, as early as 1220; he repeats the term in 1223, in the *Solet annuere* that approves the *Later Rule*. Franciscan hagiography, which on the contrary willingly forgets the term *fraternitas*, makes this transformation into the institution one of its favorite subjects, but it does so by cleverly focusing the attention on the earlier event – on the founding journey to Rome where the essential aspects would supposedly be worked out. Now, if the term "Order" did not come from Francis himself, neither was it obvious in the lexicon of the thirteenth century: Canon 13 of the Fourth Lateran Council speaks only of "the excessive diversity of religions," not of Orders.

The *Benedictine Rule*, written around 540, uses the word *ordo* to designate the liturgical office, the organization of the monastery and thus the *Rule* itself, and also Holy Orders, as Francis will also do in the *Testament*.[13] The concept of *ordo monasticus* emerges in the high Middle Ages, in the context of reflection on the classes of society,[14] as a third group alongside laity and priests, and one that is soon convinced of its pre-eminence; likewise, the expression *ordo canonicus* appears for canons. It is only beginning in the twelfth century that, in documentation coming from the Papal Curia, the term *Ordo* begins to occur frequently – often, still indistinctly associated with *religio* – to indicate what is now known as a specific Religious Order. The expression is used for Cluny in 1136 by Eugene III (1145–1153) – it had been preferable, until then, to speak of *ecclesia cluniacensis* – but in fact becomes habitual only with Gregory IX (1227–1241).

---

[13] Test 6.

[14] G. Duby, *Les trois ordres ou l'imaginaire du féodalisme* (Paris, 1978).

Citeaux benefits from this earlier, beginning in the twelfth century, as do the Carthusians.

The unique aspect of the religious institutes born at the end of the twelfth century, such as the Trinitarians, or at the beginning of the thirteenth century, like the Preachers or Minors, is that they give themselves and receive almost immediately the title *Ordo* under the meaning that is most well-known today.[15] That would certainly account for their universal purpose which is asserted very early, their pronounced centralism desired as such from the start, and their almost immediate formation into a group, as compared to the irregular pattern of new foundations made by traditional monasteries. The corollary of this new order is, in the end, the exemption from local control and the direct ties to the Apostolic See.

In 1231, the Order of Friars Minor finds itself clearly sheltered from the attacks of diocesan Ordinaries, enumerated and described at length in the flurry of letters *Nimis iniqua* and *Nimis prava* of Gregory IX, which were sent out from Rieti dated August 21, 22, 22 again and 28, 1231.[16] Concerning the direct subordination to Rome, Francis had expressed it in the previous strata of the *Earlier Rule,* promising obedience to Innocent – which thus corresponds to a version of the text previous to 1216 – and to his successors, while the friars, on their part, were bound to obey Francis and his successors.[17] The formula remains almost unchanged in the *Later Rule,*

---

[15] J. Dubois, "Ordo," in *Dizionario degli Istituti di Perfezione,* 6 (Rome, 1980), col. 806-820.

[16] *Bullarium franciscanum romanorum pontificum constitutiones, epistolas ac diplomata continens tribus Ordinibus Minorum, Clarissarum et Poenitentium a seraphico patriarcha sancto Francisco institutis concessa ab illorum exordio ad nostra usque tempora,* 1, ed. G.G. Sbaraglia (Rome, 1759), 73-7.

[17] ER Prol 3:4.

with Honorius [III] simply taking over from Innocent [III].[18] The text of 1223 also makes provision that a cardinal protector, appointed by the pope, would watch over the fate of the brotherhood.[19] It is a brotherhood that is therefore very cherished but also very controlled by its relationship with the papacy which originated in the personal relationship of its founder with the Roman pontiff.

Let us now look at the internal operation of the institution. It relies chiefly on the ministers and the chapters. The term "minister," like that of "custodian"[20] – either of which, moreover, may be substituted for the other[21] before the two terms come to indicate two very distinct levels of the hierarchy[22] – is of a clearly evangelical origin. As is proved by the frequent repetition of "minister and servant,"[23] it refers to those who are charged to maintain a government of service:

> For it must always be thus: the ministers should
> be the servants of all the brothers.[24]

The choice of this term is not a purely Franciscan invention, since the Order of the Very Holy Trinity, destined to ransom captives in the Holy Land and so innovative from an institutional point of view, had already been using it since 1198; however, it is the Order of Friars Minor that most explicitly develops the spiritual

---

[18] LR 1:2-3.
[19] LR 12:3. Also Test 33. W. Thomson, "The Earliest Cardinal-Protectors of the Franciscan Order: a Study in Administrative History, 1210-1261," in *Studies in Medieval and Renaissance History*, 9 (1972): 39-52.
[20] 1 LtCus 9.
[21] LR 8:4; RH 9.
[22] LtOrd 2 and 47; LtMin 17; LR 8:2 and 8:4; Test 31-32 and 35.
[23] ER 4, 5; LR 8:1, 10:1.
[24] LR 10:6.

content of this paradoxical terminology and assures the success of its application.[25]

At the summit is thus, "the minister and the servant of the entire brotherhood,"[26] of which, in these exact words, the *Earlier Rule* speaks only once, and this to attribute to him the role of convoking the extraordinary chapters.[27] The *Later Rule* gives him the title, fixed from that point forward, of "minister general," defines his role and reinforces his prerogatives by reserving for him the right to relieve any brother he chooses from the office of preaching,[28] while the *Earlier Rule* in 1221 grants this power to "his minister," who must be recognized as the one that in 1223 will be called the provincial minister.[29] The definitive statutory text, in Chapter VIII, describes the role and selection of the minister general in this way:

> Let all the brothers be bound always to have one of the brothers of this religion as minister general and servant of the entire brotherhood, and let them be firmly bound to obey him. At his death, let the election of his successor be held by the provincial ministers and the custodians at

---

[25] M. Conti, M. Mayeur and G. Odoardi, "Ministro," in *Dizionario degli Istituti di perfezione*, 5 (Rome, 1978), col. 1363-1369.

[26] ER 18:2. Also LtOrd 2:38; Test 27.

[27] ER 18:2.

[28] LR 9:2.

[29] ER 17:1-2. The provincial ministers will only regain the prerogative to designate the preachers in chapter through the *Prohibente Regula vestra* of Gregory IX, dated December 12, 1240. Throughout the century, a lot of dancing is done around the two questions of appointment of preachers and the absolution of serious faults, which we will not attempt to recount in detail, even if there are points which are related to our purpose; in this vein, the return to a selection of preachers by the provincial ministers certainly has some connection with the deposal in 1239 of Minister General Elias, who had exercised a very self-centered style of government.

the chapter of Pentecost, at which the provincial ministers are always required to meet, in some location predetermined by the minister general, and this once every three years or at some other interval, longer or shorter, as it will have been ordered by the said minister. And if at any time it appears to the group of provincial ministers and custodians that the said minister is not fit for the service and for the common usefulness of the brothers, let the said brothers to whom the election was entrusted be held bound in the name of the Lord to elect another as custodian.[30]

At the intermediate level are the ministers responsible for the provinces, who are already mentioned in the *Earlier Rule,*[31] and which the *Later Rule* in a straightforward manner calls "provincial ministers."[32] The *Later Rule* further specifies that they may equally be or not be priests,[33] which was to last until the generalate of Haymo of Faversham (1240-1244), according to the testimony of Pellegrino of Bologna, dated 1305.[34] Their role, according to the two preserved statutory texts, consists in receiving

---

[30] LR 8:1-4.

[31] ER 4:2.

[32] LR 2:1.

[33] LR 7:2.

[34] Pellegrino of Bologna, *Chronicon abbreviatum de successione ministrorum generalium*, ed. A.G. Little, in *Tractatus fr. Thomae vulgo dicti de Eccleston de adventu fratrum minorum in Angliam*, Collection of studies and documents on the religious and literary history of the Middle Ages, 7 (Paris, 1909), 142: "He [Haymo of Faversham] began also to reduce the status and power [*potentiam*] of the laity, who until then had held managerial positions." Cf. however Gratien de Paris, *Histoire de la fondation ...*, 152-53, who believes that this measure was taken soon after the deposal of Elias in 1239; A. Boni, "Accessibilità indifferenziata (chierici e non-chierici) agli uffici di governo nella Regola francescana," in *Apollinaris*, 55 (1982): 599-608.

postulants,[35] assigning offices to the brothers within the province, visiting them, providing them with warnings as well as encouragement,[36] correcting them when needed,[37] authorizing them to leave for the land of the non-believers,[38] and, if they wish to, convoking provincial chapters once per year, on the feast of St. Michael.[39] In the *Earlier Rule,* disobedience to a bad minister is provided for and encouraged,[40] and the minister who walks "in the flesh and not in the spirit" may be denounced by a brother to the minister general in chapter.[41]

At a lower level, the custodians,[42] who appear only in the *Later Rule,* assist the provincial ministers and participate in chapter in the election or in the potential deposing of the minister general.[43] Finally the guardians, who are however absent from the two statutory texts, complete a hierarchy which is fully deployed in the belated *Letter* known as *to the Entire Order.[44]*

As we've seen in passing, there are two types of chapters: general and provincial, even if these two terms are absent from the Franciscan writings. From the beginning of October, 1216, at a time when the religious institute had spread through all of Italy, Jacques de Vitry attests to this already well-established custom of the Friars Minor:

---

[35] ER 2:2-8; LR 2:1-10. A prerogative that, as we will see, Francis had reserved for himself until 1219.

[36] ER 4:2 and 6:1-2; LR 10:1-6.

[37] ER 5:6-8; LR 7. There are explicit disciplinary procedures in Test 30-33.

[38] ER 16:3-4; LR 12:1-2.

[39] ER 18:1; LR 8:5.

[40] ER 5:2.

[41] ER 5:4. In LR 8:4 it is the deposition of the minister general that is envisaged.

[42] 1LtCus; 2 LtCus.

[43] LR 8:2 and 4.

[44] RH 1-7; LtMin12, 14 and 17; LtOrd 47-48; Test 27-28.

Once per year, the men of this religion gather at an agreed-upon location, to their great benefit, to rejoice in the Lord and to eat together. And with the advice of good men, they write, promulgate their holy institutions and have them confirmed by the Lord Pope in holy teachings; then they disperse for an entire year into Lombardy, Tuscany, Apulia and Sicily.[45]

If we rely on the testimony of the venerable and later text of the *Passion of Saint Verecundus,* which was probably written in the second half of the thirteenth century, we nevertheless find references to the time of the beginnings and confirmation of the importance of food in these fraternal gatherings:

In the environs of this monastery [San Verecondo, on the Gubbio road], blessed Francis held the chapter of the first three hundred brothers. The abbot and the monks gave them generously whatever was necessary, as they were able. There was an abundance of bread made from barley, wheat, sorghum, and millet, fresh water to drink and apple wine diluted with water for the weaker ones – thus was it told to us by the very old Lord André, who was present there – and an abundance of beans and vegetables.[46]

---

[45] *Lettres de Jacques de Vitry,* 76.

[46] *Legenda de passione sancti Verecundi militis et martyris,* ed. M. Faloci Pulignani, *S. Francesco e il monastero di S. Verecondo,* in *Miscellanea francescana,* 10 (1906): 7.

According to the *Earlier Rule*, the chapters that afterwards are said to be general[47] must take place at Pentecost – in implicit reference to the *Acts of the Apostles* – at St. Mary of the Portiuncula, every year for the ministers from Italy, and every three years for the other ministers, unless the minister of the entire fraternity arranges otherwise.[48] It is a triennial rhythm that the *Later Rule* confirms in extending it to all the provincial ministers, always allowing however for the possibility of special assemblies if the minister general would so decide.[49] Here, the brothers who are persistently in error may be denounced;[50] here, the minister general may be elected or deposed with the participation of the custodians;[51] here, the *Rule* is completed by the addition of new clauses.[52]

The chapters on the provincial level, where all the brothers of the particular region gather around their minister, may meet each year on the feast of St. Michael, as is indicated in the *Earlier Rule*;[53] the *Later Rule* corrects this to indicate the same year as the general chapter, after the chapter.[54] It should be noted that, no matter which type of chapter or which version of the *Rule* is taken into consideration, the frequency with which they are to be held is only a suggestion, since the minister – general or provincial – can always modify it as he wishes.

---

[47] Indispensable reference to Marinus a Neukirchen, *De capitulo generali in primo Ordine seraphico*, Bibliotheca seraphico-capuccina, 12 (Rome, 1952); in deep gratitude to Aristide Cabassi for the help that he gave me throughout this research.

[48] ER 18:2.

[49] LR 8:2-3.

[50] ER 5:4.

[51] LR 8:4.

[52] LtMin 13-22.

[53] ER 18:1.

[54] LR 8:5.

The chapter is, in itself, a purely monastic tradition. It takes its name from the chapter of the *Benedictine Rule* which, as per the teaching of the Carolingian reformer Benedict of Aniane (d. 821), was to be read daily within the monastery[55] before the questions of the day, under the presidency of the abbot, are discussed. These assemblies' very practice of gathering all the monks of a house, including the youngest, to contribute to the superior's decision with their advice is present in Chapter III of the *Rule* of Benedict of Nursia and in most of the early *Rules*. In the context of a single monastery, of the same community, the question of the selection of chapter participants hardly comes up; however, it arises naturally as the number increases and becomes an issue the moment the context changes to include multiple establishments.

The concept of a "general chapter" common to a gathering of multiple houses living under the same constitutions, endowed with electoral, legislative, regulatory, administrative and judicial power, comes from Citeaux, and the first one of this type was held in 1116.[56] The Premonstratensians, the Carthusians, the monks of Grandmont, Cluny itself – intermittently from 1132 and regularly, beginning with the abbacy of Hugh V (1199-1207) – and so many other Orders or congregations were to adopt the system. As we've seen, it is based on the Cistercian model that Canon 12 of the Fourth Lateran Council imposes on all the religious houses that didn't have one, an assembly by kingdom or province, at a triennial frequency that is also recommended – with variations – in the diverse rehashings of the Franciscan

---

[55] The *Rule* is also read at the chapter of the Friars Minor: Test 37.

[56] G. Lesage, "Capitolo," in *Dizionario degli Istituti di perfezione*, 2 (Rome, 1975), col. 166-176.

Rule. But it will be discovered that, for the Cistercians, it is the abbots of the monasteries other than Citeaux who mutually determine the date of the next meeting, whereas, for the Friars Minor, this date is suggested by the regulations, but remains at the discretion of the minister general.

At first glance, the institutional machinery of the Friars Minor seems to be a happy success, in a "parliamentary" synthesis of the evangelical spirit and monastic traditions: a "legislative power" – the chapter assemblies, who name and, if needed, replace, the ministers,[57] and an "executive power" – which attends to the application of the *Rule*, the distribution of functions, and day-to-day matters.[58] There is a sharing of powers at the top, imitating the balance between council and papacy whose combination has marked the operation of the Church since the beginning. There are central organs – minister general and general chapter – and local ones, which copy the former at the provincial level. These, in turn, are divided into custodies that gather together a group of friaries according to territory.

In fact, the system, such as it appears in the legislation developed during Francis's lifetime, raises a number of perplexing issues.

The first ones are technical. To take into account only the most official of the statutory texts, the *Later Rule* states that the provincial ministers and the custodians select the minister general, but nothing specifies who is to name *them*. It is certainly a question of "an election of the successor [*electio successoris*]" to the previous minister

---

[57] D. Nimmo, *Reform and Division in the Franciscan Order from Saint Francis to the Foundation of the Capuchins*, Bibliotheca seraphica-capuccina, 33 (Rome, 1987), 34-47.

[58] Gratien de Paris, *Histoire de la fondation ...*, 149, uses the expressions "executive power" and "legislative power" in connection with the constitutions of 1239, based on those of 1260.

general, but the concrete method of this election is not determined. The allusion to the death of the minister general leads one to believe that his office is a lifetime one; yet, the duration of the provincials' office is not at all indicated.[59] The whole system may just about work if the minister takes the trouble to convoke the chapter; however, the expressions are vague in this regard: it seems, in reality, that nothing requires him to do so and, also, that nothing requires the provincial to convoke his chapter. The specific list of persons qualified to participate in or to attend the chapter of Pentecost is no longer set: the provincial ministers will certainly be obliged to go; the custodians intervene to elect or depose the minister general, but it is not known whether they are invited to the other sessions. Also unknown is if the majority of brothers are welcome or if they are asked not to come. To put it plainly, during the 1220s, the assembly may vary, according to the interpretation that one chooses to give to the ambiguities of the *Rule*, from five thousand brothers to thirteen provincial ministers!

There is another question that is "archeological." Missing from the preserved writings of Francis, the great majority of which date from the last years of his life, are the links that would ideally connect the appointment of Bernard of Quintavalle by his companions, during the journey to Rome of 1209-1210, and the text of the *Later Rule*, set down more than ten years later. How did the system refine itself? Which parts come from the founder, from the companions, from the brothers, or from the pressures or models external to the community? Was it applied from the top, by extension of the operation of the original group from Assisi through a series of districts – the provinces, then the custodies – thereby progressively organizing the Order in a systematic way? Does it also

---

[59] G. Barone, *art. cit.*

result, to some extent, from an organized grouping of experiences that in the beginning were relatively independent? Legends and chronicles will offer some clarification on this point, but this clarification would need to be completed by a series of house-by-house case studies.[60]

In the early writings, there is nevertheless an easily perceived vagueness, even in the *Later Rule* and the *Testament,* between the terms "minister," "custodian"[61] and "guardian." It is also perceived that the minister, who is not yet called "general" in the *Earlier Rule* and who is also called "custodian" in the *Later Rule*, is only the extrapolation of the minister of the smaller group of the original fraternity. One perceives also that the "ministers" who become "provincials" only in the *Later Rule* are local projections of the central superior and that the single term "chapter" applies, in both *Rules,* to both general and provincial assemblies, with no more distinction between them than the predetermined dates for their convening. In a word, we can see that the original Assisi-born model, as hesitant as it was, gained momentum and was a determining one, even and especially as soon as it had come to incorporate heterogeneous experiences.

A last ambiguity touches on the relationship between Francis and the minister general. In the *Letter* known as *to the Entire Order*, the founder is careful to address the minister general as his "venerable lord [*domino*];"[62] yet

---

[60] Let us cite for example the models given by G.M. Varanini, *Per la storia dei Minori a Verona...*; L. Pellegrini, *Insediamenti francescani nell'Italia del Duecento* (Rome, 1984); M.P. Alberzoni, *Francescanesimo a Milano nel duecento*, Fonti e ricerche, 1 (Milan, 1991); A. Piazza, *I frati e il convento di San Francesco di Pinerolo (1248-1400)*, Studi pinerolesi, 1, (Pinerolo, 1993); G.G. Merlo, *Forme di religiosità nell'Italia occidentale dei secoli XII e XIII* (Verceil-Cuneo, 1997), 177-94.

[61] 1LtCus and 2LtCus seem still to be addressed to all superiors, not to those of a specific rank.

[62] LtOrd 2 and 38.

he nevertheless does not deprive himself of giving him orders: to have the *Rule* observed, always to have the present missive with him and to put it into practice.[63] There is the same pattern in the *Testament:* a declared intention to obey on Francis's part – "and I wish firmly to obey" [*Et firmiter volo obedire*][64] – but an imperatively required obedience to his last wishes from the minister and from all the other leaders – "let them be bound by obedience" [*per obedentiam teneantur*].[65]

In a word, in the light of the writings, one has the feeling that the founder was not greatly concerned for the institutional operation of his community and that, despite his repeated protestations of submission, reserved for himself the right to intervene in the name of his spiritual authority, seeking to extend its effects beyond the time of his own death.

THROUGH THE LEGENDS

As we continue to follow the same two related themes – ministers and chapters – let us turn our attention to the early legends – The *First Life* and the collections issued by the command of the Chapter of Genoa and of the Minister General Crescentius of Jesi in 1244. Contrary to what the most rigorous method would dictate,[66] they will be used here as needed, insofar as each of their specific identities has already been defined elsewhere.[67]

Right away, to dispel the risk of philologic-combinative artifice, let us simply bring up the following: that the *First*

---

[63] LtOrd 40 and 47.
[64] Test 27.
[65] Test 35.
[66] J. Dalarun, *The Misadventure*, 36-37 and 139-141.
[67] J. Dalarun, *The Misadventure*.

Life, written by Thomas of Celano in 1228-1229, has as its main purpose to clarify the relationship between Francis and the Apostolic See, with keen attention to the role played by Cardinal Hugolino who, having meanwhile become Pope Gregory IX, presided at the canonization of the Assisian in July 1228. The *Anonymous of Perugia*, written by Brother John in 1240-1241, and the *Legend* known as *of the Three Companions*, completed in 1246 by Brothers Rufino and Angelo, grant a singular importance to the internal organization of the Order – in particular to chapters and provinces. The *Legend of Perugia*, reflecting the information gathered by the companions and especially by Brother Leo between 1244 and 1246 and the *Second Life* that Thomas of Celano completes in 1246–1247, inspired by the earlier collection from the companions, place the emphasis on the leadership and then on the resignation of Francis and on the intentions which guided each one.

In other words, like all paths that one attempts to follow through the Franciscan hagiographical maze, the theme of the exercise of government comes to reveal the specificity of each of the legends and to bring out the basic differences that divide them by groups: the *First Life* focuses on the relationships of Francis and the Order with the Church. John, Rufino, and Angelo are chroniclers of the brotherhood that is becoming an Order – at least as much as hagiographers of the founder. Leo and the *Second Life*, which is influenced by him, concentrate on "the Franciscan drama."

But let us take up again the thematic thread of our particular interests: founder and ministers, provinces and provincials, cardinal protector, chapters.

The *Second Life,* clearly, teaches us in what spirit Francis bore the title of minister general:

Humble in his behavior, more humble in his thought, the most humble in his estimation of himself. One could not perceive that this prince of God [*Dei princeps*] was a prelate [*praelatus*], if it weren't for this luminous jewel: that he was the most insignificant among all the lesser ones. It is this virtue, this title, this sign that indicated that he was Minister General.[68]

In keeping with the *Legend of Perugia* from which we have already cited the account, Thomas of Celano also relates the resignation of Francis which results in Peter Catanii's succession[69] (which probably occurred on September 29, 1220 – that is, seven days after the institution of the novitiate by the *Cum secundum*, the absence of which had shocked Jacques de Vitry in the spring of 1220). Several episodes from the legends present us with a founder who has resigned, who is submissive and obedient to the new minister general as well as to the provincial ministers,[70] seeing a doctor when his superior orders him to do so.[71] Some of the disobedient acts of the saint are completely to his credit, such as when he gives away his tunic despite having been forbidden to do so by his successor and his guardian.[72] Sometimes, he makes use of a permission which does not fail to be granted by Peter Cattani, but it is to carry out exemplary acts, by forcing his successor to allow him to engage in penances of his choice: to share the food of a leper from his bowl, to be led naked through the city of Assisi with his cord

---

[68] 2C 140.
[69] LP 76, 87 and 105; 2C 143, 151 and 188.
[70] 1C 169; 2C 151 and 207; LP 106.
[71] 1C 98; LP 42 and 46.
[72] LP 52.

around his neck, covered in ashes, while admitting that he had eaten meat.[73]

However, other passages prove that the founder continues, without hesitation, to command the minister general.[74] It is especially obvious that it is Francis, with no form of collegiality or even consultation, who designates both Peter Cattani – "the first minister general whom he himself had chosen"[75] – as well as, upon his death (on March 10, 1221), Brother Elias to succeed him. Lastly, the founder who had resigned, if certain accounts are to be believed, could not refrain from disparaging the unfortunate one who had been propelled into his place.[76] It is of course Elias, and not Peter Cattani, who must be recognized as this successor that the narrators leave anonymous. That there is a desire here on the part of the hagiographers – Leo in his *Legend of Perugia* and Thomas of Celano in his *Second Life,* when they write in the 1240s – to devalue an Elias who had returned as minister general from 1232 to 1239 and who since that time had been deposed and excommunicated,[77] even though the same Thomas of Celano had shown him in a better light in the *First Life,*[78] is only too obvious. But one may wonder if a tirade like this one, taken from

---

[73] LP 22 and 39.

[74] LP 56 and 91; 2C 67.

[75] LP 39. Also LP 105; 2C 143 and 184.

[76] LP 76; 2C 184-186, 188 and 193.

[77] G. Barone, "Frate Elia," *Bullettino dell'Istituto storico italiano per il Medio Evo e Archivio muratoriano,* 84 (1974-1975): 88-144; Ead., "Frate Elia: suggestioni da una rilettura" in *I compagni di Francesco e la prima generazione minoritica. Atti del XIX convegno internazionale, Assisi, 17-19 ottobre 1991* (Spoleto, 1992), 59-80.

[78] 1C 108-109. J. Dalarun, "La dernière volonté de saint François. Hommage à Raoul Manselli," *Bullettino dell'Istituto storico italiano per il Medio Evo e Archivio muratoriano,* 98 (1986): 161-99; Id., *The Misadventure,* 59-75.

the *Legend of Perugia*, doesn't also convey something of Francis's real feelings:

> As long as I was in charge of the brothers [*officium fratrum*] and the brothers remained faithful in their vocation and profession – even though at the beginning of my conversion to Christ I was very ill – with my little solicitude I, through my example and preaching, was enough for them. But when I saw that the Lord was daily multiplying the number of brothers and that these, through a lukewarm spirit and lack of fervor, began to deviate from the straight and secure way that they had followed until then, to take [...] a wider road, respecting neither their profession, nor their vocation, nor the good example, when I realized that neither my teaching nor my example could make them abandon the path that they had taken, I placed the religion of the brothers into the hands of God and of the ministers. Yet, although at the time when I gave up the responsibility of the brothers and resigned from this post, I excused myself before the brothers at the general chapter, arguing that I could not care and be solicitous for them because of my illness, nevertheless, if the brothers walked and had continued to walk according to my will [*secundum voluntatem meam*], I would not want, for their consolation, for them to have any other minister but myself until the day I die. [...] However, until the day I die, I will not cease teaching my brothers, by my example and by my actions, how to walk on the path that the Lord showed to me and that I, myself, showed to them and of which I informed them,

so that they have no excuse before the Lord and that, later, I am not bound to give an account of them nor of myself before God.[79]

It is a rumination full of bitterness that the *Second Life* summarizes by this terrible cry:

"Who are they," he asked, "these who have snatched my religion and the religion of my brothers from my hands? If I come to the general chapter, then I will show them what my will is [*qualem habeam voluntatem*]!"[80]

One can only wonder again at the anguish conveyed by these words attributed to Francis:

At one time, as the chapter of the brothers that was to be held near the church of St. Mary of the Portiuncula approached, blessed Francis said to his companion: "I would not consider myself a lesser brother if I did not have the attitude that I am going to describe to you." And he said: "Imagine that the brothers, with great devotion and veneration, come and find me and invite me to the chapter, and, touched by their devotion, I go to the chapter with them. And once we are all together, they ask me to proclaim the word of God among them, and, rising, I preach to them as the Holy Spirit inspires me to. Suppose that after this sermon they think it over and rise up against me, saying: 'we no longer want you to rule over

---

[79] LP 76.

[80] 2C 188. In the dialog that follows, it appears that Francis is aiming at the provincial ministers who remain in charge too long and who think of their functions as being hereditary.

us [*regnare super nos*].[81] You have no eloquence at all; you are too simple-minded and we are too ashamed to have a simpleton and one worthy of such contempt as superior [*prelatum*]. From now on, do not claim to call yourself our superior!' Then, heckling me, they drive me away.... And so! I would not consider myself a lesser brother if I were not just as joyful when they vilified me and ashamedly rejected me, refusing that I be their superior, as when they honored and venerated me, provided that both scenarios were equally advantageous for them. For, if I rejoice over the benefit they receive and their devotion when they exalt and honor me – which may be dangerous for my soul – how much more must I rejoice over my gain and the salvation of my soul when they revile me by ashamedly rejecting me – which is beneficial to my soul!"[82]

Lastly, one cannot fail to note, in the most objective way possible, that, even though he successively named two minister generals to replace him, it is Francis who writes the greater part of the *Later Rule*,[83] that it is still "Brother Francis" individually – three years after his resignation – that Honorius III addresses in his *Solet annuere* to approve the definitive *Rule* in 1223,[84] and that it is again he who, in Chapter I of the *Later Rule*, guarantees, by the personal obedience he promises to the pope, the very fundamental link that unites the Order to the Roman See.[85]

---

[81] Lk 19: 14.
[82] LP 83; Also 2C 145.
[83] LP 113; LMj 4:10.
[84] G.G. Merlo, *Intorno a frate Francesco. Quattro studi,* Presenza di san Francesco, 39 (Milan, 1993), 97-102.
[85] LR 1:2. R. Brooke, *Early Franciscan Government* ..., 106-18.

The *Anonymous of Perugia* and the *Legend of The Three Companions* relate how, "eleven years after the beginning of the religion," ministers were sent "into almost every province of the world where the Catholic Faith is reverenced;"[86] also, the date for the creation of provinces is remembered as being in 1217.[87] From reading the same sources, it would seem that the superiors in question, forerunners of the provincials, "were elected ministers [*electi fuerunt ministri*]" in these circumstances.[88] But, as we have already said, we must be cautious about the meaning of the verb *eligere*, which generally indicates an outcome without giving much information regarding the procedure followed: the *First Life*, incidentally, indicates that it is Francis who named certain ministers to head a province.[89] The *Anonymous of Perugia* points out the power attributed to them to receive postulants,[90] but the *Legend of Perugia* attests that the founder does not hesitate to tell them what to do or to set his authority against theirs.[91] Several passages from the *Legend of Perugia* and from the *Second Life* – as would be expected – openly present them, as a group, as enemies of Francis and of his evangelical project, attempting to diminish the interpretation of poverty, to favor the possession of books, neglecting to insert in the *Rule* the respect due to

---

[86] AP 44; L3C 62.

[87] On the evolution of the provinces, Gratien de Paris, *Histoire de la fondation* ..., 522-26; J.R.H. Moorman, *Medieval Franciscan Houses* (New York, 1983), 691-92; L. Pellegrini, "I quadri e i tempi dell'espansione dell'Ordine," in *Francesco d'Assisi e il primo secolo di storia francescana,* 166-201.

[88] AP 44; L3C 62.

[89] 1C 48 (*a sancto Francisco minister fratrum in Provincia constitutus*) and 77.

[90] AP 45. This piece of information matches what is in the *Rules,* but, as we will see, Francis reserved this prerogative for himself until 1219.

[91] LP 32, 69, 71 and 74; 2C 62, 187 and 188.

the writings which carry the name of the Lord, fearing that the founder is concocting a piece of legislation that is too difficult, and hanging on to their offices as if they were a hereditary right.[92]

> "The brother ministers think they will make light of God and of me?" And he added: "Well! So that all the brothers know and are warned that they are bound to observe the perfection of the Holy Gospel, I wish to have written at the beginning and at the end of the *Rule* that the brothers are bound to observe the Holy Gospel of our Lord Jesus Christ."[93]

From such passages, innumerable references to a government of service in Francis's writings in the last years of his life are made to appear in another light: as if they are really more of a warning against shifts in observance than a simple statement of the original ideal?

The legends provide more of an understanding of the role of the cardinal protector of the Order, an office officially entrusted to Hugolino, Cardinal Bishop of Ostia, the future Gregory IX, by Honorius III in 1220.[94]

This person is very important and he is intimately linked to both the history of the institutionalization of the Friars Minor and to the formulation of the similar feminine experiences at the monastery of San Damiano as well as in the entire Order of the same name. Born into the family of the Conti de Segni, Hugolino was related to Innocent III. His education is essentially a juridical

---

[92] LP 69, 80, 112 and 113; 2C 188.
[93] LP 69.
[94] 1C 99-101; AP 43 and 45; L3C 61 and 63-67; 2C 25.

one, giving him the facility with which he handled the drafting of normative texts. Appointed Cardinal of St. Eustache by Innocent III in 1198, then Bishop of Ostia in 1206, he leads various legations on behalf of the Apostolic See: to Germany in 1207-1209, to attempt a reconciliation between the two pretenders to the throne, Otto of Brunswick and Philip of Swabia; to Northern and Central Italy in 1217, to pacify local rivalries, and in 1218, to bestow the imperial authority on the young Frederick II (1212–1250). This last one is an irony of history, considering the conflicts that afterwards set him against his one-time protégé and which marked his long pontificate, from 1227 to 1241.

Before the time of his official nomination as Cardinal Protector of the Order of Friars Minor in 1220, Hugolino, who must have taken up the task in this domain from Cardinal John of St. Paul who died in 1216, watched unofficially over the destinies of the nascent religious institute. He attends the general chapter of Pentecost[95] and dissuades especially Francis, at the time of the meeting in Florence in 1217, from going to France at a time when, it seems, the cardinal was not yet persuaded of the universal vocation of the Umbrian Experience.[96] He became protector of the Order, he guides the relationships between the Apostolic See and the founder, introducing him to Pope Honorius III and the cardinals.[97] He ensures good relations between the brothers and bishops of various regions where the Order is spreading rapidly.[98]

Several legends – the *First Life* more than any other – testify to the affection that bound the saint and

---

[95] AP 43; L3C 61.
[96] 1C 74-75; LP 82. R. Manselli, *St. Francis of Assisi* (Chicago, 1988), 187-199.
[97] 1C 73.
[98] L3C 62 and 66.

Hugolino,[99] a piece of information that there is no reason to question. But for the most rigoristic brothers, who in fact rediscover the echoes of ascetical writings and monastic traditions, the cardinal represents the world – indeed a worldly Church.[100] It is evident that he plays a moderating and normalizing role with Francis. Such is certainly the case in 1221, when, to calm the anger of the Poverello at the idea that the Minors could own their own dwellings, he declares himself proprietor of the house of the Bologna friars,[101] or again when the learned brothers – probably in 1222 – persuade him to act as an intermediary to bring the Order back towards the well-established *Rules*.[102]

The *Anonymous of Perugia*, chronicle of the institution-alization, concerns itself especially with chapters. Francis, shortly after his interview with Innocent III, would have set their frequency at two per year: at Pentecost and at the feast of St. Michael,[103] initially held at St. Mary of the Portiuncula.[104] The following is the description of one of these assemblies:

> At Pentecost, all the brothers [*omnes fratres*] met in chapter near the church of St. Mary of the Portiuncula. At this chapter, they would discuss how they could better observe the *Rule*. They divided the brothers into different provinces, so that they could preach to the people and introduce new brothers into their provinces. For his part, Saint Francis admonished and reprimanded the brothers and enacted precepts [*praecepta faciebat*],

---

[99] 1C 74 and 99-101; LP 42 and 46.
[100] LP 33 and 61; 2C 63.
[101] 2C 58.
[102] LP 114.
[103] AP 36; L3C 57.
[104] 1C 78; AP 37; LP 11 and 79; 2C 57 and 63.

as it seemed good to him to do so, after having consulted with the Lord [...] As the chapter ended, he blessed all the brothers present at the chapter and sent each into the province that he wished.[105]

The *Anonymous of Perugia* repeats again the reduction of the frequency of the chapters between the *Earlier Rule* and the *Later Rule*, to avoid displacing the brothers living in far-off countries too often.[106] It tells of several successive chapters with the sending of missions,[107] but nothing indicates exactly which brothers attended: beyond the required presence of the ministers, it really seems that for a long time the assemblies remained open to everyone[108] – hence the great throng at the chapter of Mats in the early 1220s (probably at Pentecost of 1222), assessed at five thousand brothers by the *Legend of Perugia*. This is moreover one of the rare occasions, in the legends previous to Bonaventure, in which the qualifier "general" appears attached to "chapter."[109] At these assemblies, they speak of the lives of the holy Fathers,[110] they discuss the *Rule*, and, above all, they pass their time in listening and listening to Francis, who speaks uninterruptedly, enacting the precepts that must govern the life of the brothers.[111]

---

[105] AP 37-40. Also L3C 57-59.

[106] AP 44.

[107] AP 45.

[108] LP 71.

[109] LP 114. The combination "general chapter" appears neither in 1C, nor in AP, nor in L3C, nor in 3C. On the other hand, it is present in the writings of Julian of Speyer, *Vita s. Francisci*, 75 (regarding the chapter of 1230), in LP 76 and 114, and in 2C 188. The imaginary "general chapter" of 2C 191-192 brings together all the religious of the Church. The term has evidently become standard in LMj.

[110] L3C 59.

[111] LP 2 and 7; 2C 128 and 200.

Allusions to chapters held in the provinces are more rare. Hagiographers nevertheless insist on showing that, while the founder is not able to attend all the local assemblies, his spirit hovers over each one of them and he knows the secrets of the heart. This is just what is proved by the episode at the Chapter of Provence, told in the *First Life* and taken up again with insistence by Bonaventure, who situates it in Arles.[112] It is a chapter at which Anthony of Padua is also presented and which the *Chronicle of the XXIV Generals*, written around 1369 by Arnold of Sarrant, dates to 1224.

> Just as, at one time, Brother John of Florence had been appointed by Saint Francis as minister of the brothers in Provence and when he was celebrating the chapter of brothers in the aforementioned province, the Lord God, in his usual mercy, opened the door of eloquence for him and made all the brothers willing and attentive listeners. There was among them a brother priest of great reputation and an even more holy way of life, named Monaldo. His virtue was founded on humility, supported by frequent prayer, and protected by the shield of patience. Also present at this chapter was Brother Anthony, whose mind the Lord had opened so that he would understand the Scriptures and pour out upon all the people words about Christ that were sweeter than honey from the honeycomb. Now, while he was preaching to the brothers with all his heart and in a manner full of faith on the theme "Jesus of Nazareth, king of the Jews," the aforesaid Brother Monaldo glanced toward the door of the house where the brothers were all assembled. He

---

[112] LMj 4:10.

saw there, with his physical eyes, blessed Francis raised up in the air, with arms extended in the form of a cross, blessing the brothers. Everyone seemed to be so filled with the consolation of the Holy Spirit and, strengthened by the salutary joy that they had thereby conceived, they willingly believed what they heard concerning the vision and the presence of their most glorious father.[113]

The hagiography of Anthony of Padua, for its part, will be in no hurry to take up this piece. And for good reason: here the lone and omnipresent hero is Francis – a saint who immediately puts into action what the preacher attempts to explain through the use of words, a founder whom nothing escapes and who irradiates the entire Order, its entire system, with his Christ-like presence.

As far as institutional arrangements are concerned, the legends are therefore hardly any more explicit than the writings. The chapters that are only belatedly called "general" seem in the beginning to have been conceived – at least until the early 1220s – as a form of "direct democracy" of the group of Friars Minor, functioning at a relatively high rhythm. The increasing number of members, the remoteness of a part of this militia caused by the creation of provinces that are ever more distant, and the isolated nature of Assisi at that time, in comparison to an Order in the process of expanding to the dimensions of Christianity, certainly reduced their frequency. Certainly the chapters that will be called "provincial" took up the task in part, not without the suspicion hanging over them of favoring the

---

[113] 1C 48.

centrifugal forces within the community. If the writings and legends are brought together, it must be imagined that, even if the general chapters were open to all the brothers without distinction, the provincial ministers had a singular influence there, since it was known that, along with the custodians, they were the only ones who had the power to intervene in decisions as serious as the election or the deposition of the minister general. Yet nothing determined their own appointment. What is more, nothing seemed to guarantee any representative position of these persons, who most often were certainly appointed in a discretionary manner by the founder.

The ministers' actions, like those of the chapters, are in practice indeed limited by the influence of Francis's personality. His counsels supposedly coming from God, he finds himself the possessor of a charismatic authority that legitimated a very personal exercise of legislative as well as executive power, which his resignation of 1220 did not radically call into question. It would be tempting to say: on the contrary. Thus, counter to the generally accepted ideas that would rather show a Francis exploited by the papacy in the service of a universal ecclesial and pastoral plan, the reading of the sources allow us without difficulty to establish a different picture. They show us that it is really Francis who, beginning in 1209–1210, kept pushing to get himself placed under the direct authority of the Apostolic See, very probably in contradiction to the wishes of the Bishop of Assisi. They also show us that it is he who, in 1217, desired to take his religious institute outside of Italy, having already reached its limits the preceding year, as is testified to by Jacques de Vitry, and spread it beyond the Alps. In doing so he provoked the temporary reservations of Hugolino and, behind him, of the Roman Curia. It is again Francis who certainly selected the two minister generals who successively replaced him, which did not prevent him from being notably identified as the addressee of the papal letter confirming the *Later Rule* in 1223.

That such a way of acting provoked internal conflicts is obviously not emphasized in the legends written to glorify the saint; however, certain passages allow it to be understood between the lines. It is worth wondering, then, if the resignation of 1220, traditionally presented as a gesture of supreme humility, was not also a sort of emotional blackmail of the Poverello's – a double thrust. On the surface, he seems to say: "you'll have to manage without me; I don't want to know any more about it." At a deeper level, he seems to say: "why criticize my use of power, since I have renounced it?" In any case, it is certain that the founder's withdrawal from the exercise of government was a very theoretical withdrawal, which proceeds from a loss of his influence over the brothers and is more a show than a statement of fact, which therefore makes no dent at all in his thirst for influence and in no way hinders – far from it! – his attempts to intervene directly in serious matters. Lastly, it is necessary, in the logic of this hypothesis, to reconsider the *Testament* itself, the one out of all Francis's texts that most overwhelmingly makes appeals to Providence. Just as the founder attempted to protect his authority beyond his resignation precisely by the grace of his resignation, the dying man in the same way certainly tried, through the superb text where the story of his beginnings introduces his last wishes in a summary that is graphic and powerfully effective in all respects, to protect beyond his death a part of what death was going to take back from him.

Through the Chronicles

Two chronicles especially illuminate the beginnings of the Order and include the points of view that interest us: those of Jordan of Giano, the Italian native who describes the expansion of the friars in Germany, and of Thomas of Eccleston, who relates the same phenomenon in his native country, England.

Not that it is necessary to pass over Salimbene de Adam in silence. This citizen of Parma, accepted as a novice on February 4, 1238 into the Order of Friars Minor by Brother Elias in person – of whom he will later speak so ill, with a fury that can only have arisen from disappointment or great vexation – is, like Jacques de Vitry, an indefatigable traveler and an insatiable busybody. From an excellent educational background and fiercely aristocratic ideology, in the course of his wandering between Italy and France, he meets the Emperor Frederick II, of whom he is a warm supporter, Bernard of Quintavalle and Hugh of Digne who, he says, introduce him to Joachimite speculations, Louis IX (1226-1270), and the Minister General John of Parma (1247-1257). He is ordained to the priesthood in 1248 and settles in to complete his studies at Reggio Emilia. His *Chronicle*, which has come down to us only through a single manuscript preserved at the Vatican Apostolic Library, written by the author himself, and partially destroyed, narrates the events that unfold from 1268 to 1287; it was written from 1283 to 1285, then added to until 1288.[114] It is unquestionably one of the largest sources of information on the thirteenth century. But precisely: it wanders off in so many directions, alternating digressions, inserted treatises, flashbacks, leaps and bounds, great reflections on the way the world

---

[114] O. Guyotjeannin, *Salimbene de Adam: a Franciscan Chronicler* (Turnhout, 1995).

works and small settlings of scores, that we do not deprive ourselves of frequently calling on him for help; yet, for all that, we do not offer it as a systematic study.

Jordan is a man of a more discreet manner. He comes from Giano, a small mountain village near Montefalco, in Umbria. A deacon, he embraces the form of life of the Friars Minor probably in 1219. In 1221, following a misunderstanding that he recounts with inimitable humor, he takes part in the first mission sent to Germany: Salzburg, Speyer, Worms, Mainz.... In 1223, he is ordained a priest, and appointed guardian of the friary in Mainz in 1224. Then he leaves for Thuringia, where he establishes the Order and resides until around 1239. In 1241, he is very likely to have been vicar of Bohemia and Poland, then, from 1242 to 1243, vicar of Saxony. He resurfaces only in April 30, 1262 at the Chapter of Halberstadt, aged and enfeebled.

It is on this same day that our author begins to dictate his *Chronicle,* in order to preserve the memory of the beginnings of the Friars Minor in Germany. But he reveals himself to be extremely attentive also to the overall institutional operation of the Order, which he then continuously details at this double level: general operation and application in the German provinces. Two works – the Berlin manuscript, finished in the second half of the fourteenth century, and the Karlsruhe manuscript, resurfacing only in the fifteenth century, – are both incomplete, but nevertheless complement each other to present the text of the *Chronicle* of Jordan of Giano, which Nicholas Glassberger and Jean de Komerowski, observant compilers of the first half of the sixteenth century, will use extensively.

Jordan is an affable man, full of humor, with an exalted opinion of obedience, level-headed, an astute diplomat, and valued by all who meet him. That is why, on the whole, he should be trusted. Now he doesn't hesitate to say, as we saw at the outset, that until 1239, Elias, "indeed held the entire Order in his power [*habuit totum Ordinem in sua potestate*], just as blessed Francis and Brother John Parenti had before him."[115] For Jordan – implicitly, for he doesn't express himself clearly on this point – Peter Cattani and Elias were thus only vicars of the founder, who, like his two direct successors, reserved for himself a power that could rightfully be described as absolute over the destiny of the Order and the friars.

Around 1223-1225, and therefore definitely after the resignation of 1220, Jacques de Vitry, in his *Histoire occidentale (Western History),* also testifies to the complete and respectful obedience of the "junior priors [*minores priores*]" and of the other brothers to the one that he calls their "supreme prior [*summum priorem*]"[116] and who is none other – as is later discovered – than Francis himself.[117] In the *Cum secundum* of September 22, 1220, Honorius III had made the same blunder in addressing the "priors or custodians of the Friars Minor." There is therefore a contradiction between the choices displayed by the founder, who on no account desired the title of "prior" within the Order[118] and who claimed to have abandoned all power in 1220, and the image that his government presented to contemporaries and left to immediate posterity.

In the *Chronicle* of Jordan of Giano, examples abound of this limitless power. In 1219, says our author (in fact, more probably in 1217), it is Francis who decides on the

---

[115] Jordan of Giano, *Chronica*, 61.

[116] Jacques de Vitry, *Historia occidentalis*, 32, ed. J.F. Hinnebusch, *The Historia occidentalis of Jacques de Vitry*, Spicilegium friburgense, 17 (Fribourg, 1972), 159.

[117] Jacques de Vitry, *Historia occidentalis*, 161-62.

[118] ER 6:3.

missions to France, Germany, Hungary, and Spain, and who designates who will go.[119] It is he who appoints the various provincial ministers.[120] Between the chapters of 1217 and the 1221 Pentecost "general chapter" [121] all the terms that we are familiar with are established. All the brothers, professed and novices – three thousand in all, the *Chronicle* proposes[122]– attend the great assembly which takes place at St. Mary of the Portiuncula.[123] But it is the founder who convokes the chapter[124] and who influences all the important decisions. Peter Cattani is not even named as vicar and Elias is nothing but Francis's spokesman. Francis, at the feet of his vicar, pulls him by the tunic to give him instructions as the general chapter progresses. The very manner in which the founder is called "the Brother" – "that signified the blessed Francis

---

[119] Jordan of Giano, *Chronica*, 3.

[120] Id., *ibid.*, 9.

[121] The *Chronicle* speaks of May 23, 1221: this is an erroneous date, since Pentecost fell on May 30 in 1221.

[122] LP 114 and Thomas of Eccleston, *Tractatus fr. Thomae vulgo dicti de Eccleston de adventu fratrum minorum in Angliam*, 6, ed. A.G. Little, Collection d'études et de documents sur l'histoire religieuse et littéraire du Moyen Âge, 7 (Paris, 1909); English translation in *XIIIth Century Chronicles: Jordan of Giano, Thomas of Eccleston, Salimbene degli Adami.*, ed. and translated from the Latin by Placid Hermann, OFM (Chicago, 1961), 1-77, speak of five thousand brothers. This is certainly not the same chapter, since in LP 114, Hugolino is present, whereas, with Jordan, it is Cardinal Rainaldo; Thomas, for his part, makes an allusion to the chapter where the destruction of the brothers' house recounted in LP 11 took place. Be that as it may, for this, the early 1220s, the number put forward by Jordan of Giano is plausible. Hence the formidable problems of the food supply; Marinus a Neukirchen, *De Capitulo generali ....*, 400-01. The friars certainly numbered twenty thousand around 1280, and more than thirty thousand at the beginning of the fourteenth century; G. Miccoli, *Il Testamento ...*, 734-35. As a basis for comparison, the Friars Preacher would have numbered four thousand in 1237, eight thousand in 1277 and ten thousand in 1303.

[123] Jordan of Giano, *Chronica*, 16.

[124] Id., *ibid.*, 15.

who was called in this way by the brothers, as being the brother *par excellence*"[125] – points to a charismatic authority that is out of control. In the determination of each one's mission, certainly there is some form of fraternal discussion: volunteers are raised up,[126] and the one in charge of an operation is asked with whom he wishes to associate;[127] but, if all else fails – as was cruelly experienced by our poor author, when he was forced to leave for Germany – if it isn't Francis, it is Elias who calls the shots.[128]

At the provincial level, the minister of Germany Caesar of Speyer has at his disposal, as is provided in the *Rule,* an identical discretionary power for receiving new brothers,[129] sending some here and others there, recommending brothers to the priesthood, appointing custodians,[130] and calling recalcitrants to order, even if he has the wisdom to be able to repent of his abuses of authority.[131] The first provincial chapters, which brought together all the brothers of a region, testify to the success of the German mission: around thirty in 1221,[132] the friars, beginning in 1222, fill up one of the two choirs of the Cathedral of Worms.[133] But it is obvious, when Caesar is replaced in 1223 by Albert of Pisa as the head of the German province, that this decision comes from the Assisi General Chapter and not at all from any vote of the friars of the province.[134] At two levels, general and

---

[125] Id., *ibid.*, 17. Also Id., *ibid.*, 12, Peter Cattani's response to Francis: "You have the power (*potestatem*)."
[126] Id., *ibid.*, 18.
[127] Id., *ibid.*, 19.
[128] Id., *ibid.*, 18.
[129] Id., *ibid.*, 25.
[130] Id., *ibid.*, 24, 28 and 30.
[131] Id., *ibid.*, 27.
[132] Id., *ibid.*, 23.
[133] Id., *ibid.*, 26.
[134] Id., *ibid.*, 31.

provincial, the chapter seems thus to function only as the counsel, in the vassal-like sense, in the Benedictine sense also, of the person who presides over it – indeed as a simple rubber-stamp.

The arrival of Albert of Pisa in Germany changes none of these practices.[135] The institution of custodies and guardians[136] are so many administrative adjustments dictated by the expansion into Germanic soil; this expansion moreover necessitates the restriction of the provincial chapters to only custodians, guardians, and preachers, beginning in 1224.[137] But it will be understood that these managers of sub-districts, of friaries and of the pastoral ministry, who assist the provincial minister in all the appointments and transfers,[138] are not at all commissioned to represent their brothers of the "rank and file." Flowing from the summit, a veritable management apparatus is rapidly set up, which alone is "in charge." And it takes the exasperating humility of Brother Nicholas of Erfurt, who, in 1225, refuses the office of custodian of Saxony, to make Albert of Pisa fly off the handle and force him to recall that the responsibilities in the Order are only "burdens and servitude" [*onera et servitutes*].[139] One year before the disappearance of the founder, this essential Franciscan fact had clearly ceased to be obvious.

Upon Francis's death in 1226, Elias, whom Jordan until then considers only as vicar of the founder, convokes a chapter to elect the new minister general – which, it must be admitted, gives some legitimacy to our chronicler's point of view. According to the provisions of the *Later Rule*, only provincial ministers and custodians

---

[135] Id., *ibid.*, 38 and 49.
[136] Id., *ibid.*, 32, 33 and 47.
[137] Id., *ibid.*, 37 and 51.
[138] Id., *ibid.*, 37.
[139] Id., *ibid.*, 49.

are affected.[140] Warned of this convocation, Albert of Pisa himself brings about a chapter of custodians, guardians, and preachers in the German province. Far from soliciting the opinion of the local assembly on the decision that he is going to have to make, the provincial minister decides on the friars who will accompany him to Assisi.[141] There, contrary to all expectations, John Parenti (1227-1232) is elected minister general at the general chapter of 1227.[142] He continues to make appointments to all the offices of the Order,[143] including the various provincial ministers necessitated by the dividing up of the province of Germany that began in 1230.[144] In 1229, he institutes visitators[145] that were also provided for, as will be remembered, by Canon 12 of the Fourth Lateran Council, who are most probably in charge of ensuring the suppression of particularist tendencies. Elias, returning as minister general in 1232, takes up this innovation for himself.[146]

1209 to 1239 are thirty years of a continuously autocratic exercise of power, within a highly centralized and hierarchical organization. These years are marked by two major crises. The intention here is not to launch into the Order's history of events, but these tremors interest us insofar as, like all crises, they allow us to test the solidity and the relevance of the institutions, and make modifications where called for, on the surface or in depth.

The first crisis occurred during Francis's journey to the East, in 1219-1220. When leaving Italy (around the

---

[140] Id., *ibid.*, 50.
[141] Id., *ibid.*, 51.
[142] Id., *ibid.*, 51.
[143] Id., *ibid.*, 52 and 54.
[144] Id., *ibid.*, 57-58.
[145] Id., *ibid.*, 56.
[146] Id., *ibid.*, 61.

summer of 1219), he had appointed two vicars, Gregory of Naples and Matthew of Narni, who were delegated to receive new brothers in his name – a decision which until then had been his responsibility alone;[147] the preserved *Rules* of 1221 and 1223, henceforth granting this prerogative to the provincial ministers, offer no hint of this practice prior to their establishment. The vicars, relying on a chapter of elders – here, as on a few other occasions, the need is felt to appeal to an implicit legitimacy of the eldest[148] – seek most probably to normalize the Order along the lines of monastic tradition, in particular regarding the fasts. The fact that it is a lay brother who comes to denounce the guilty ones to Francis[149] encourages the thought that the forces rendering the Order a more monastic and more clerical one were already working hand-in-hand in this reorientation given to the Order that was putting Italy in turmoil. The *Cum secundum* of September 22, 1220, which institutes the novitiate year, certainly comes from the Papal Curia, but odds are that even before the founder's return, it was prepared there in close connection with the vicars.

The absence of the leader, all the more a charismatic leader, is always a serious problem when no precise provision exists that governs a delegation of power. Francis reacts by a resumption of control taken with determination and an expertise that is surprising for this adherent of the refusal of power:

---

[147] Id., *ibid.*, 11.
[148] Id., *ibid.*, 11, 32 and 63.
[149] Id., *ibid.*, 12.

> There, having understood completely the
> cause of the disturbances, he went, not to the
> troublemakers, but to the Lord Pope Honorius.[150]

Indeed, in reading Jordan of Giano who surprisingly says no word either of the Assisian's resignation or of Peter Cattani's ephemeral vicariate who must nevertheless have replaced Matthew of Narni and Gregory of Naples, we seem to understand the following: that the appointment of Hugolino as Cardinal Protector at the founder's express request addressed to Honorius III,[151] the copying out of the *Earlier Rule* – Francis "reformed the Order according to his own statutes"[152] – and the convocation of the 1221 general chapter of Pentecost[153] are so many means put in play to avert any move of the community away from the strict wishes of the founder. Of course, we know furthermore that Francis resigned just after returning from the Holy Land, probably on September 29, 1220, which as we can imagine is not unrelated to the issue of the *Cum secundum* one week earlier, which must have made him consider that he'd had enough. But it is even more striking that this episode in no way contradicts Jordan's account, that nothing changes, on either side of this unannounced caesura, in the attitude of a founder who really wants, again and always, armed with the repeated support of the Apostolic See, that his wishes be commands. The 1221 chapter, where Francis, unwell and lying down, pulls Elias by his tunic to inform him of his inspired wishes, is the very expression of this attempt to restore order.

---

[150] Id., *ibid.*, 14.
[151] Id., *ibid.*, 14.
[152] Id., *ibid.*, 15.
[153] Id., *ibid.*, 15-16.

The same crisis therefore has two possible interpretations: it could be seen as the Poverello valiantly resisting those who would have wanted to alter completely the purity of the new Franciscan movement; or it could be seen as his obstinate refusal of any initiative, of any proposition that he did not suggest or that did not follow his way of thinking. These two interpretations, when looked at closely, are not so contradictory. It is the papacy that holds the key to the apparent contradiction, since it abandons the short-lived vicars to seal a new alliance with the contested founder who is bypassed by his own. Perhaps Honorius III and his entourage understood at that time that, for the good of the Church, another monastic Order would never fulfill the promise of the new Franciscan movement. Let us then allow the other main protagonist of the conflict's settlement to speak for a moment, with this excerpt from the *Vie de Grégoire IX (Life of Gregory IX)* which, whatever the views of those who believe in Francis as an ethereal dreamer, is perhaps not just papal propaganda:

> [Gregory] also put the Order of Minors, which in its beginnings wandered on an uncertain path, in the right direction by the instruction of a new Rule [*novae Regulae traditione direxit*]; and he gave form to the formless [*informavit informem*], by assigning blessed Francis to them as minister and rector.[154]

The second big crisis, according to Jordan of Giano, breaks out in 1239 and is directed at Brother Elias, who manages distinctly less well than his master. In 1232, the general chapter, which for the first time – if the

---

[154] *Vita ejusdem Gregorii papae IX ex cardinali Aragonio*, ed. L.A. Muratori, *Rerum italicarum scriptores*, III, 1 (Milan, 1723), 575.

Chronicle is to be believed – had been held in Rome and no longer in Assisi,[155] had dismissed John Parenti and substituted Elias for him, in a posthumous return to the wishes of the saint who had been officially canonized July 16, 1228. Jordan of Giano clearly indicates that the absolutism of the new minister general, appointing offices in all authority, was only a continuation of the governments of Francis and of John Parenti.[156] But Elias goes too far, by never convoking the chapter[157] and by making more appointments of visitators who were to be unconditionally subject to his views.[158] Beyond the problem of the Order's basic direction, which cannot be appropriately discussed here, Elias's tactical error is not to have known how to use the general chapters, those convenient rubber stamps, as safety valves allowing the display – in the absence of real representation or true deliberative power – of a semblance of pseudo-collective consultative expression. An apparent confirmation of the minister's decisions by the assembly – perhaps the latter would not really have discussed them – that was a safe bet – but it would in any case have made them indisputable. The pressure mounts and the reaction occurs around 1239:

---

[155] Thomas of Eccleston, *De adventu*, 13, situates this chapter in Rieti where Gregory IX then resided. Either place indicates a papal influence.

[156] The *Chronica generalium ministrorum Ordinis fratrum minorum,* in *Chronica XXIV generalium Ordinis minorum cum pluribus appendicibus inter quas excellit hucusque ineditus Liber de laudibus s. Francisci fr. Bernardi a Bessa*, Analecta franciscana, 3 (Quaracchi, 1897), 216, specifies: "the minister general then indiscriminately instituted and dismissed provincial ministers, minister's custodians and guardian custodians and used others to do his bidding."

[157] Jordan of Giano, *Chronica*, 61.

[158] Id., *ibid.*, 62.

Having held a council, the brothers decided
to provide in common [*communiter*] for the
Order.[159]

For the first time, a power conflict between the
minister general and the community of brothers
– or, at least, the brothers who claim to represent the
community and who, to explicitly mention Alexander
of Hales and John of La Rochelle, are masters of the Paris
studium – thus breaks out headlong. The logical statutory
solution would have been to depose the minister in
general chapter, as provided for in the *Rule*.[160] Now we
can understand why Elias, if he could tell which way the
wind was blowing, failed to convoke such a meeting!
After a fruitless appeal against a visitator that the friars
of Saxony had made to the minister general, the logical
canonical solution is an appeal to the pope who, as the
pontiff himself specifies, "absorbs all appeals."[161] There
is a new meeting of the friars, who carefully write up
their grievances and inform the pontiff of them. A
committee of twenty wise men is formed to draft the
constitutions that the Order so grievously lacked.[162] From
this standpoint the friars are behind the other religious
institutions of the time. A general chapter is convoked
at Rome in 1239, almost certainly on the initiative of
Gregory IX. It is obviously not a coincidence if the work
of the preparatory committee, later approved by the pope
and by the general chapter, provides "that the choice of
ministers, custodians, and guardians will be made in a
different way from that observed until now."[163] Faced

---

[159] Id., *ibid.*, 61.
[160] LR 8:4.
[161] Jordan of Giano, *Chronica*, 63.
[162] Id., *ibid.*, 64.
[163] Id., *ibid.*, 65. *Chronica XXIV generalium*, 246 reports that, on
becoming minister general, Haymo of Faversham "wished that his

with autocracy, the first solution that came to the friars' minds consisted of reconstructing the pyramid from its base.

The reaction came to a great extent from the brothers involved in the Parisian university life. On the slopes of St. Genevieve Mountain, these Minor scholars had had the opportunity to form friendly ties with the Friars Preacher, whom they esteemed, admired and sometimes almost envied.[164]

As a basis for comparison, but also because this model may have influenced the conference conducted in 1239, let us recall that the Order of Friars Preacher is organized, according to the *Constitutions* that are drawn up from 1216 to 1237 to supplement the *Rule* of Saint Augustine, in an indisputably more precise and communitarian manner than the Order born from the works of the "new fool in the world." The conventual prior is elected by the friars of the area for a limited length of time. The election is confirmed by the provincial prior, who is himself elected by the provincial chapter. The province's chapter meets every year, gathering the conventual priors, the preachers, and – elected by the friars as a kind of opposition force – as many definitors as priors. The provincial chapter designates the provincial definitors and the visitators. A general chapter takes place every year at Pentecost. For two years in succession, it gathers the provincial definitors; the third year, it is the provincial priors who are in session. But, at whatever point one is

---

power [*potestatem*] be as limited as that of the provincial ministers and the custodians by the general chapter. And then the custodians lost the power to institute and to dismiss the guardians of the friaries." This shift appears in fact more characteristic of the measures taken in 1239 than of those that will come to correct the first ones in 1242.

[164] J. Dalarun, "Francesco nei sermoni: agiografia e predicazione," in *La predicazione dei frati dalla metà del '200 alla fine del '300. Atti del XXII convegno internazionale, Assisi, 13-15 ottobre 1994* (Spoleto, 1995), 365-66.

situated in the cycle, the general chapter, independently of its composition has unaltered powers. The master general is elected for life by the general chapter, which also confirms the provincial priors. Each superior can be deposed by his immediate superior in the hierarchy, except the minister general, who can be dismissed by the general chapter.[165]

Let us return to the Friars Minor and to Jordan of Giano. The same general chapter of 1239 deposes Elias, replaces him with Albert of Pisa (1239-1240)[166] and changes the boundaries of the provinces.[167] From here, the *Chronicle* accelerates its account, as if, from this point on, our author were only interested in showing the harmonious operation of an Order at last governed in a collective way, according to rules that were clearly defined, known by all and respected: election of the provincial minister by the assembly of friars from the province[168] or, if this election is still by the minister general, it is based on a preliminary delegation from the provincial chapter;[169] smooth deposings, in general chapter, of two successive minister generals – Crescentius of Jesi[170] and John of Parma.[171]

If we really think about it, moreover, the fate of the minister generals and of the vicars, from Francis to Bonaventure, was all in all chaotic: Francis resigned in 1220, Peter Cattani died in 1221, Elias was not confirmed

---

[165] D.E. Showalter, "The Business of Salvation: Authority and Representation in the Thirteenth-Century Dominican Order," *The Catholic Historical Review*, 58 (1973): 556-74.

[166] Jordan of Giano, *Chronica*, 66.

[167] Id., *ibid.*, 67.

[168] Id., *ibid.*, 69.

[169] Id., *ibid.*, 71.

[170] On the radical criticism of all authority in the Order by the *solemnes fratres* during the generalate of Crescentius of Jesi, M. Cusato, *La renonciation ...*, 504-19.

[171] Jordan of Giano, *Chronica*, 76 and 77.

by the Assisi Chapter in 1227, John Parenti was replaced by the Rome Chapter in 1232, Elias was deposed at Rome in 1239, Albert of Pisa and Haymo of Faversham died in office in 1240 and 1244, Crescentius of Jesi and John of Parma were dismissed by the general chapter in 1247 at Lyons and in 1257 at Rome respectively. The initial institutional negligence has the effect – a predictable one when all is said and done – of engendering repeated crises: six out of nine transitions; and also two of the superiors who died in office had had extremely short generalates. Haymo of Faversham is truly the only one to have triumphed over the office and over time. But precisely, Jordan seems to tell us, there is no comparison between the almost insoluble conflict of 1239 and the normal exercise of the prerogatives of the general chapter in 1247 and 1257. The good institutions are those that overcome crises; the better ones, those that absorb them.

Striking is the fact that the *Chronicle* ends unobtrusively with an event that can seem trivial. Nevertheless, the work of Jordan of Giano is not one of these day-to-day accounts embellished with each day's unexpected occurrences, ending haphazardly with the chronicler's death. Rather, it is really a memoir, dictated as a whole to Brother Baldwin of Brandenburg.[172] The end therefore makes sense.

On April 29, 1262, Conrad of Brunswick is dismissed in chapter from his office as minister of the Saxony province. His successor, Brother Bartholomew, although absent from the meeting, "was elected of one accord [*concorditer*] and was confirmed on the spot by Brother Conrad in the name of the minister general[173] – proof of the *fair play* of which – Thomas of Eccleston tells us

---

[172] Id., *ibid.*, Prol.
[173] Id., *ibid.*, 78.

– Elias was truly incapable after his defeat of 1239.[174] It is not surprising that this Bartholomew is in fact the silent partner of the *Chronicle!*[175] However, in reading Jordan of Giano, there is also the feeling that, by the account of this real election, technically irreproachable, ratified by the one defeated – an election which, of course, requires the endorsement of the minister general, but nevertheless establishes the assembled friars' power of recommendation – our author gives us something important. He provides us – more than the flattery of an old man to his new superior – the conclusion of a tortuous process whose crises endangered the Order and which consisted in nothing other than the institutional translation of the very long work of a mourning that the charismatic founder would have wanted to be never-ending.

Just about nothing is known of Thomas of Eccleston – not even the meaning of the place-name that a seventeenth-century pen joined to his name. Entering the Order of Friars Minor between 1229 and 1232, he must have studied at Oxford and composed his chronicle from 1231-1232 to 1257-1258. It is a true chronicle, therefore, that is nevertheless known under the title of *The Coming of the Friars Minor to England.* Four manuscripts – two incomplete ones from the second half of the thirteenth century that are in fact the remnants of the same codex, and two almost complete ones from the beginning of the fourteenth century – of which none are the original, bear witness to Brother Thomas's text. The institutional operation of the Order interests him, but less directly than Jordan of Giano. The question of the construction of friaries and of the rapid expansion of studies demands more of his attention. Let us simply

---

[174] Thomas of Eccleston, *De adventu,* 13.
[175] Jordan of Giano, *Chronica,* Prol.

pick out a few confirmations or details in comparison with the preceding account.

At the beginning – meaning from 1223 to 1239 – the friars, to organize their community life, had nothing but the *Rule* and "a very small number of other statutes that were issued at the beginning of the very year that the *Rule* was ratified."[176] In saying this, Thomas of Eccleston is almost certainly aware that the system is very weak in comparison to many Orders of the era; however, unlike Salimbene de Adam who in retrospect sees that as an obstacle to the sound operation of the Order,[177] he seems to consider that it did not initially pose a problem.

From reading the English chronicle, it is again obvious that the minister generals appoint the provincials in a discretionary manner: Francis names Agnellus of Pisa in this way as minister of the province of England in 1224, as John Parenti afterwards designates the minister of Ireland.[178] Haymo of Faversham (most probably after his election in 1240 by the general chapter gathered at Anagni) did not hesitate to depose and imprison Gregory of Naples, the provincial minister of France.[179] All appointments naturally come from the superiors and this offends no one.[180] The provincial minister himself

---

[176] Thomas of Eccleston, *De adventu*, 5. The bull *Quo elongati*, issued by Gregory IX on September 28, 1230, goes very much in this direction since it brings up, on the subject of the friars' attitude with regard to monasteries of monks, an elucidation of Chapter XI of the *Later Rule* "by the means of a certain constitution of the same era as the *Rule*, while Francis was still alive, by the provincial ministers [...] in general chapter;" "Die Bulle *Quo elongati* Papst Gregors IX.," ed. H. Grundmann, *Archivum franciscanum historicum*, 54 (1961): 24. On the first traces of statutes in the Order C. Cenci, "De fratrum minorum Constitutionibus praenarbonensibus," *Archivum franciscanum historicum*, 83 (1990): 50-52.

[177] Salimbene, *Cronica*, ed. G. Scalia (Bari, 1966), 145-47.

[178] Thomas of Eccleston, *De adventu*, 1.

[179] Id., *ibid.*, 6.

[180] Id., *ibid.*, 4.

appoints friars to offices in his area.[181] Sometimes the
superior consults a friar about his destination, but it
is considered polite, for the latter, to leave it up to
obedience.[182] It is within the remit of every official to
appoint his temporary replacement who vaguely bears the
title of vicar, but not to have an influence on the choice
of his successor. Elias, in 1235-1236, becomes indignant
that Agnellus of Pisa, feeling death approaching, had
thought it good to propose to him the names of three
brothers to succeed him and he deliberately waits for a
year to make his decision..., even though he ends up
keeping one of the three suggested names. We must wait
for Haymo of Faversham's generalate to see a provincial
minister from England truly elected – unanimously it is
true, which always makes us a little uncertain what to
think. But, an even more daring idea: the confirmation
of this choice, which always canonically constitutes the
real appointment, comes from the electorate itself.[183]

Thomas of Eccleston clarifies the way the general
chapters are run. It is evident that the meetings open to
all – such as the Assisi General Chapter in the early 1220s
where Francis orders the destruction of the friars' house,[184]
five thousand participants strong, says our chronicler[185]
– are characterized by confusion and, consequently,
are subject to the schemes of those who convoke and
manipulate them. In 1230, counter to the provincials'
opinion that the *Rule* designated them, together with
the custodians, as the only electorate, Elias infiltrated
his supporters into the general chapter that was being
held at Assisi, in the hope of deposing John Parenti

---

[181] Id., *ibid.*, 12.
[182] Id., *ibid.*, 1.
[183] Id., *ibid.*, 14.
[184] Cf. LP 11.
[185] Thomas of Eccleston, *De adventu*, 6.

and of taking his place.[186] At least that is how Thomas
of Eccleston presents it. But if it is clear, according to
the terms of the *Later Rule*, that the power to elect the
minister general falls only to provincials and custodians,
nothing is said specifically of the right to participate in
the general chapter and it really seems that the practice,
at least until 1222, was to welcome all the brothers. Is
Elias defending a certain conception of the community,
or is he above all aiming for power? If such is the case, he
redeemed his defeat of 1230 by his victory in 1232. But
his experience must have warned him against general
chapters because he realized he could manipulate them
only in the "demagogic" way – in the etymological sense
– that he got from his master, and provided that there
is a crowd. Salimbene tells us that in 1239, faced with
the chapter convoked by the rebel ministers, the general
again dreamed of nothing other than summoning the
lay brothers there – his strongest friends – counting on
the striking and convincing force of their bludgeons. The
pope put things to rights, in limiting the meeting to the
categories provided by the *Rule*;[187] this is for the election
of the minister general, of course, for it is really the only
case where a restriction is indicated by the statutory text.
After Elias's dismissal, the reduction of the provinces to
thirty-two is justified by Thomas of Eccleston in this
way:

> Given that the election of the minister general
> depended solely on the ministers and the
> custodians, if there had been too great a number of
> votes in the election or the deliberation, since the
> multitude is cause for confusion, it would hardly

---

[186] Id., *ibid.*, 13.
[187] Salimbene, *Cronica*, 232-33.

have been possible to settle business requiring the consent of so many persons.[188]

The chronicler tells us also of the failures of institutional development. We have already seen that the visitators instituted by John Parenti, who were to hold chapter in the various provinces and submit everything to the minister general, saw their powers excessively increased by Elias, which brought about his downfall. The untimely visits in England and in Ireland indeed prompted the appeal to the pope, the brothers recognizing the right of the visitators to inspect only if invested by and having the authority of the general chapter.[189] Thomas of Eccleston, confirming Jordan of Giano who already cited the names of two Paris masters, specifies that the "savage" general chapter that met against Elias was mainly made up "of provincial ministers and very wise friars from this side of the Alps."[190] Salimbene, in a corroborating way, indicates that Elias sometimes gathered the ministers from Italy, but never the others, fearing that they would depose him.[191] The gap, cultural above all, which then widened between the peninsula and countries like Germany, France and England, is certainly a cause in the development of the crisis. Thomas of Eccleston specifies that the preparatory committee at the following general chapter was composed of elected friars.[192] Likewise, after the pope had deposed Elias to the delight of the great majority – not of all however[193] – our author makes a point of giving these details on the election of the successor:

---

[188] Thomas of Eccleston, *De adventu*, 9.
[189] Id., *ibid.*, 8.
[190] Id., *ibid.*, 13.
[191] Salimbene, *Cronica*, 232.
[192] Thomas of Eccleston, *De adventu*, 13.
[193] Id., *ibid.*, 15.

The pope, then entering alone into a cell, called the ministers and the custodians to hold the election. And before they had written it, he heard each one's vote; and when Brother Albert of Pisa, minister of England, was canonically elected and the election was announced, Brother Arnulf, penetentiary, who had principally led the whole affair, intoned *Te Deum laudamus*.[194]

"Canonically elected" indeed, since Gregory IX takes care to respect the spirit of the provisions of the Fourth Lateran Council's Canon 24, which provided, as is recalled, that three trustworthy persons designated by the electorate, for whom the pontiff here substitutes himself, gather the votes "in secret and one by one" and put them down in writing before announcing the results. But it is easy to imagine the weight that must have been carried by the pope, who is not the first teller to come, flanked by his penitentiary who made use of a good office – one foot in the Curia, one foot in the Order.

The visitators, expression of autocratic centralism, were an instrument fatal to the minister general. But the definitors erred in the opposite way and brought about the ruin of their own chapter. Thomas of Eccleston places their introduction under the generalate of Haymo of Faversham (1240-1244).[195] The minister general had known the Friars Preacher for a long time, and he had had the opportunity to value their company at the University of Paris; moreover, he had converted to the life of the Minors around 1224, in the company of three other academics, his friends, only after having requested the advice of the general master of the Order of Preachers,

---

[194] Id., *ibid.*, 13.
[195] Id., *ibid.*, 13.

Jordan of Saxony.[196] On the model of the Dominican *Constitutions*, the Minors' definitors, chosen by the friars apart from the superiors, were to represent an organ of the executive's control, a role that the chapter theoretically could not fill as long as the provincial ministers were designated by the general. But the first meeting of the chapter of definitors seemed too clearly turned against the provincial ministers and against the general himself. It was the last one; also being abolished at the same time was the statute providing for the canonical election of the guardians and custodians. In fact, after these unsuccessful attempts, it is at the one general chapter, meeting alternately on one side then on the other side of the Alps according to a measure taken – as our chronicler tells us – by the Minister General John of Parma (1247-1257), that the role of deliberation and of surveillance will return within the Order.[197]

On this point, Thomas of Eccleston must be supplemented and corrected by the much later *Chronicle of XXIV Generals*. The institution of definitors almost certainly goes back to the *Constitutions* of 1239 and it is in reality their first chapter that is to take place under Haymo, hence Thomas's error. In any case, what appears clearly through his account is that Haymo of Faversham is in fact the true guide of the Order, from the rebellion of 1239 until his death in 1244. The *Chronicle of XXIV Generals* allows the first meeting of the chapter of definitors to be situated at Montpellier (in 1241); but it also cites – in contradiction with Thomas of Eccleston who spoke of a same first and last meeting of the type – a chapter of definitors at Bologna (in 1242).[198] Taking into account the two sources, the tendency would be to

---

[196] Id., *ibid.*, 6.
[197] Id., *ibid.*, 13.
[198] *Chronica XXIV generalium*, 247.

think that the Montpellier Chapter is indeed the first and only one where the definitors (or more precisely, a party from among them, namely the "discreet" friars elected by the provincial chapters to the exclusion of the provincial ministers) attempted to hold a separate chapter, on the model of the Preachers and that the Bologna Chapter was the first to gather "discreets" and ministers in a "new system" of general chapter. But we must understand as well that the Montpellier Chapter was a general chapter, since the definitors attempted to drive the ministers away from there. The composition of those present is thus really the same in 1241 and 1242, but, with one year between them, two systems confront each other: separate chapters, according to the mode that attempted to impose itself, brutally, in 1241, and a combined chapter, according to a model which prevails from 1242.

Let us not hold his few moments of imprecision against our English chronicler. This would be unfair with regard to this engaging account, which is also capable of showing us brothers shivering with hunger and cold, trying to warm themselves by sharing a drop of beer diluted in warm water![199] Less set in a quasi-teleological account of the institutional evolution than Jordan of Giano, Thomas of Eccleston is nevertheless a first-prize witness, because he also helps one understand the entire context of these events: differences in geographic areas, in status between priest and lay brothers, in levels of culture. In the final analysis, Thomas's great merit is that he reminds us that there is never a problem that is in itself institutional.

---

[199] Thomas of Eccleston, *De adventu*, 1.

THROUGH THE NORMATIVE TEXTS

Nevertheless, we really must return to the normative texts to understand the outcome of this torturous story. The documents taken into consideration here will be of three types: papal letters addressed to the Order – those that dealt with our question, of course – , *Constitutions* of the Order adopted in general chapter, and *Commentaries* of the *Rule* closely tied to this statutory elaboration[200] – twelve texts in all. The set time limit will in theory be that of the *Constitutions* of Narbonne, promulgated in 1260. However, to respect the coherence of the *Commentaries'* genre and to find that which, in the latest of these texts, might clarify the earlier conceptions or developments, we will continue in that respect up to the treatise of Angelo Clareno, written in 1321-1322.

On September 28, 1230, Gregory IX, from Anagni, addresses a letter "to the minister general and provincial ministers and to the custodians and to the other brothers of the Order of Minors" – the *Quo elongati*.[201] The pope in this way responds to the list of demands submitted to him by a delegation composed of the minister general (therefore John Parenti) and the provincial ministers who had previously met in chapter. We must deduce that this means the Assisi General Chapter at the end of May, 1230. Through Thomas of Eccleston, we know that Anthony of Padua, Girard of Rossignol, Haymo of Faversham (already!), Leo of Perego, Girard of Modena and Peter of Brescia had been sent to the Sovereign

---

[200] Clear presentation of D. Flood, *Peter Olivi's Rule Commentary. Edition and Presentation*, Veröffentlichungen des Instituts für europäische Geschichte Mainz, 67 (Wiesbaden, 1972), 92-103; also Id., "The Order's Masters: Franciscan Institutions from 1226 to 1280," in *Dalla "sequela Christi"*, 41-78; A. Tabarroni, *art. cit.*, 93-122.

[201] "Die Bulle *Quo elongati*," 20-25.

Pontiff.[202] These demands, which we know only by the pope's response, principally affect the *Rule* – a *Rule*, recalls Gregory IX, which the *Testament* exhorted not to gloss and whose first commentary he is nevertheless going to give here, thus inaugurating a slightly embarrassed plea for the clarification of the founding text which all authors will have to carry out after him.

By appealing to the good of souls, using his familiarity with Francis and his role in the composition of the *Later Rule* during the time when he was Cardinal Protector, Gregory first indicates to the brothers that they are not bound by the content of the *Testament* for two reasons:

> Without the consent of the brothers and the ministers in particular – because that concerned everyone – he [Francis] could not obligate and he did not obligate in any way his successor, for the equal does not have power [*imperium*] over his equal.

The criticism – a sharp one – places itself at a two-fold level in the past: during his lifetime, the Assisian did not consult the chapter to compose this piece of writing, as he should have done, it is understood, for a restrictive normative text; what is more, he attempts to impose his point of view beyond death, which is not compatible with the strict respect of his successors' authority. For the pontiff, the founder here is only one minister general among others – the first, certainly, but equal to the ones who follow in the chain of succession. Is this a betrayal of the last wishes of Francis, as most people say?[203] Or

---

[202] Thomas of Eccleston, *De adventu*, 13.
[203] D. Flood, "The Politics of the *Quo elongati*," in *Laurentianum*, 29 (1988): 370-85.

is it a desire to deliver the community of brothers from an indisputable and timeless charismatic authority, abusive particularly in that? That will be determined. In any case, Gregory IX seized perfectly upon the absence of dialog and the unlimited will to impose his views that characterized the humble and gentle Poverello. He moreover suggests, in an implicit manner, that the *Rule's* worth lies not in that it was dictated by the saint, but in that it was ratified by a general chapter.

The other points of the *Quo elongati* have to do with respect for evangelical principles, the use of money, ownership of houses, confession of the brothers, examination of preachers, the powers of the provincial ministers' vicars, and visits to monasteries of nuns. One of the pontiff's recurring preoccupations seems to be to see that the scope of the minister general's activities is not diminished, neither from above by the residual effect of the *Testament*, nor from below by pressure from the majority of the friars. Far from imagining the difficulties that the successor of John Parenti will bring him in 1239, he still believes in an Order that is kept firmly in hand by its leader, as his *Life* claims that he had wished for Francis himself. If the reasoning is done in terms of function and not of people, there is continuity and coherence in the attitude of Gregory IX.

That is why the minister general must henceforth see his power freed from the weight of the statute of the Commendatore that the very memory of the founder constitutes. And only the pontiff could take away this obstacle which weighed on all the friars: both by the power to unbind which is the right of the holder of the keys of Peter – and that especially concerns the *Testament* – and also by the reminder of the relationship of intimacy which united Francis and Hugolino – and that principally concerns the *Rule*. In the final analysis, to achieve his aim – that is to say, a removal of the mystique from the saint's wishes –, the pontiff himself must paradoxically claim a legitimacy drawn from his familiarity with the charismatic founder and from his ability to uncover his intentions. Regarding the modes of the minister general's election in chapter, the delegation had asked if it was agreed that all the custodians should be present beside the provincial ministers:

> We respond that the custodians from the many provinces invest [*constituant*] one among them whom they send to the chapter with their provincial minister to represent them [*pro ipsis*], delegating their votes to him. [*voces suas committentes eidem*].

Here again, there are two ways to think about this first attempt at explaining the Franciscan *Rule* that the intervention of Gregory IX constitutes. If the content of his responses is examined, it is tempting to see there so much of a watering down in comparison to the original ideal. If the modes of operation of the Order of Friars Minor are examined, it would be concluded that the pontiff was concerned that it be a viable organization – one that is alive and not the reliquary of a dead founder. One cannot fail to take note of the first very clear expression of the principle of representation and of delegation in the history of the Order. And again, one may wonder about the meaning of this measure: is it restriction of access to elective power, or the putting into play of conditions allowing the proper management of such an election? To set the correct limits to this innovation, let it suffice however to recall that the custodians were in no way either elected, or representatives of the brothers from the custody, since they were appointed by the provincials.

Is Gregory IX's response in the *Quo elongati* mainly that of a cold jurist's, attempting to deal with the evangelical inspiration of the *Testament*? Certainly, but the brothers' demands were themselves of a strictly juridical nature. They had to learn to live without the inspired founder, and the preservation of the ideal which they had received from him would pass from then on through forms of law.

In 1239, the Rome General Chapter – the very one which carried out the deposing of Elias and his replacement by Albert of Pisa – also produced legislative work. Salimbene emphasizes the fundamental importance of this:

> And in this chapter a very great number of *General Constitutions* were made, but they were not orgnized; Brother Bonaventure, Minister General, put them in order afterward and he added there little of his own devising, although in some places he prescribed the tariff of penances.[204]

The *Constitutions*, in most religious Orders, are normative texts that complete the *Rule*, clarify its gaps, update its requirements, and give it a particular coloring. Long considered lost, these *Constitutions* of 1239 were in large part rediscovered by Cesar Cenci, in a text written by a thirteenth-century hand, in two columns on a double-leaf palimpsest of parchment contained in the composite manuscript 529 of the Bibliothèque Casanatense of Rome, in folios 25-26.[205] Between the

---

[204] Salimbene, *Cronica*, 233.

[205] C. Cenci, "De fratrum minorum Constitutionibus praenarbonensibus," *Archivum franciscanum historicum*, 83 (1990): 50-95. This codex of II-46 f. contains the *Legenda aurea* of Jacques de Voragine and the legends of Anthony of Padua and of Clare of Assisi, transcribed on paper by fourteenth-century hands; it formed a whole with the ms. 1712 of the Casanatense, where the *Legenda aurea* and the legends of Anthony and of Clare continue. In the ms. 529, two double leaves of parchment were joined together: the first one (f. 25-26), which inter-

text brought to light by the publisher, unfortunately partially destroyed at the beginning and the end, and the proposals for the reconstruction of the missing parts by Luigi Pellegrini,[206] it is possible to propose an analysis of the 1239 *Constitutions*. This may be done as long as preference is always given to the oldest text and recourse to the *Constitutions* put in order by Bonaventure during the Narbonne Chapter of 1260[207] – those very ones to which Salimbene makes allusion – is made only for the provisions missing from the double leaf but which can be cautiously assumed to have been present in the original text.

A first series of articles must have dealt with "the general chapter," which is easily understood when the historical situation is taken into account. The very fact that the assembly revives its legislative function in 1239 – at least it didn't inaugurate it! – emphasizes its importance as the exclusive source of law within the Order. However, we can surmise the original provisions concerning the chapter – completely absent from the Casanatense double leaf – only from the Narbonne text, but not without risk of anachronism.[208] The *Rule*, we

---

ests us, and the second one (f. 27-28) which is composed of excerpts of statutes from the Chapters of Pisa (1263) and of Argentan (1282). This collection, just like the ms. 1159 of the Biblioteca Oliveriana de Pesaro that also contains excerpts of decisions from various general chapters of the decades 1260-1280, belonged to Brother Ranutius de Montone.

[206] L. Pellegrini, "Introduzione," in San Bonaventura, Opusculi francescani/1, Sancti Bonaventurae Opera, 14/1 (Rome, 1993), 28-33.

[207] "Statuta generalia Ordinis edita in capitulis generalibus celebratis Narbonae an. 1260, Assisii an. 1279 atque Parisiis an. 1292," ed. M. Bihl, *Archivum franciscanum historicum*, 34 (1941): 37-94 and 284-319.

[208] *Ibid.*, 309-313. For clarity of presentation, in this section as in the following ones, the rubrics and titles of the *Constitutions* of Narbonne, absent from the 1239 *Constitutions*, are used. On the other

are told, left the minister general too great a latitude for convoking general chapters; he will henceforth not be able to space them more than three years apart. They will take place alternately on either side of the Alps – here precisely is a point which, according to the testimony of Thomas of Eccleston, as we recall, goes back only to the generalate of John of Parma (1247-1257) and which therefore could only originate from the text of 1260, not that of 1239; we cite it here only as a caution. Coming from each province will be the provincial minister escorted by a single companion – a traveling companion, that is, whose number must be limited to avoid an uncontrollable crowd in the city chosen for the holding of the chapter –, a custodian chosen by the other custodians (according to the directives of the *Quo elongati*) and a "discreet" friar chosen by the provincial chapter. In anticipation of his absences, the provincial will designate his vicar with the counsel of the discreet friars; the custodian will do likewise. The brothers coming without being summoned to the place where the chapter – general or provincial – is being held will be expelled from there. Elias's attempts at infiltration have not been forgotten! The "definitors" of the general chapter are the "low-ranking [*subditus*]" ministers and brothers – the "discreet" friars specifically chosen by the provincial chapter – who will however not participate in the election or the deposing of the minister general, which is reserved for provincials and custodians by the *Rule*. The "discreets," it goes without saying, are those who display that medieval virtue *par excellence*: *discretio* – discernment. The term is first a moral one before it takes on an institutional meaning.

---

hand, the preference will be to follow the order of the themes and articles such as it appears in the double leaf.

It must therefore be understood that the general chapter is of one rule for some and of another for the rest: provincials and representatives of custodies intervene in what concerns the minister general; provincials and friars chosen by the local chapters "define" the decisions that involve the Order.[209] On the whole, all categories taken into account, the assembly can be estimated at some one hundred forty persons.[210] In the deliberations, "the opinion of the majority [*sententia plurium*] systematically prevails." The chapter meets at Pentecost. The minister general must first of all accuse himself of his faults, and then leave the meeting-place. The provincials and custodians then remain closed up in conclave, without food. Each one in turn may express his grievances against the general; if there is a matter for discussion, it is put down in writing and the interested party, who has the right to present his defense, is notified. Each one votes "as if in an election" and it is then determined if the minister general must be corrected or dismissed. The decision is made by absolute majority plus one vote – "according to the opinion of the part greater than half of all [*iuxta sententiam maioris partis medietate omnium*]." If the general must be dismissed, he will be, whether he likes it or not. The election of the successor must be done as quickly as possible, overnight. Once the fate of the minister general is thus determined, for better or for worse, the chapter at last begins its work – and it must be imagined that at this moment the custodians cede the place to the discreet friars – with the consideration of questions coming from the provinces and the presentation of the current situation in each of them. The assembly provides for the offices of lectors and preachers, for missions to the non-

---

[209] Excellent summary in Marinus a Neukirchen, *De capitulo generali* ..., 227-28.

[210] Id., *ibid.*, 259-60.

believers, and for transfers from one province to another. It is also the chapter that chooses the place of its next meeting.

Another series of articles, this time partially preserved in the Casanatense double leaf, deals with "elections of ministers."[211] Missing from here are the clauses on this theme that occur first in the *Constitutions* of Narbonne. Inasmuch as the double leaf presents a text whose beginning is missing, it is logical to assume that they were present in the oldest version. First defined is the procedure for the election of the minister general. The "tellers [*disquisitores*]" gather and write down the votes of the provincials and the custodians in front of everyone. The ballot must be announced immediately. If everyone by divine inspiration agrees on the same person, so much the better; if not, the one on whom the votes of more than half of the electorate will have fallen will be elected. In case no majority prevails after two ballots, the decision will be put to three or five wise friars, who will act "on behalf of all [*vice omnium*]." As we see, this is nothing other than the strict application of Canon 24 of the Fourth Lateran Council. The procedure will be the same for the provincial ministers, elected by the friars in provincial chapter and confirmed by the general. However, if the friars have not made their choice the second day of the meeting, the decision falls to the minister general, unless the provincial is elected by the whole Order (in general chapter, it must be assumed). In the event of the minister general's death, the procedures are carefully laid out: if he dies before the feast of Saint Michael, the general chapter will be convoked for the following Pentecost; however, if he dies after September 29, there will be no modification of the date previously

---

[211] "Statuta generalia Ordinis," 292-95; "De fratrum minorum Constitutionibus praenarbonensibus," 67-9.

scheduled for the holding of the assembly. The provincial of the place where the chapter occurs presides at it, just as it falls to the custodian in the district from which the provincial dies to convoke the provincial chapter to elect a new minister and a vicar (who, it must be inferred, will be in office until the confirmation of the provincial). It is understood that all of these provisions continuously aim at warding off the most pressing danger: in the event of the deposing of the general, the chapter is already canonically called together and things must happen quickly to avoid all indecision. In the event of a sudden death, it is advisable to make sure of a comfortable delay in convocation, which shields the decision from all contention.

A new series of articles, completely preserved in what remains of the original version, deals with "visits in the provinces."[212] Each one of them is to be covered every three years by a visitator designated by the general chapter (as was provided by Canon 12 of the Fourth Lateran Council), assisted by a "discreet" friar. The visitator, who can be neither minister, nor custodian, nor lector, must travel to all the province's houses and rectify the publicly-known errors, but must be careful not to investigate those that remain hidden. Each brother must point out his errors to him and respond to the inquiry about the errors of others, but must be very careful not to make any wild accusations. The visitator corrects the guilty ones, in front of the provincial chapter, if necessary, but apart from the provincial minister. In the event of an entire province's resistance, the matter is transferred to the general chapter. Visitators must observe absolute silence on that which they have discovered and rectified. If they commit some excess, the provincial chapter may appeal to the general chapter.

---

[212] *Ibid.*, 69-75.

One series, limited to three articles in the Casanatense double leaf, deals with "the provincial chapter."[213] Yet, it is likely that the main points of this theme – we remember that Salimbene emphasizes the disorder of the 1239 measures in comparison to those of 1260 – would originally have been brought up, in direct connection with the clauses concerning the general chapter, at the beginning of the document. This would explain the loss of most of the information, which is therefore necessary for us to reconstruct here mainly from the *Constitutions* of Narbonne. A chapter must be held annually in each province. The custodians and brothers come to it, but it's better to limit the number of participants. Each of the brothers does not have a vote, but, on the other hand, each friary designates a "discreet" friar to send to the chapter. One therefore notes here a remnant of "direct democracy" reduced to what is possible for everyone. What is not encouraged – that everyone attend the assembly – is dealth with by the implementation of "indirect democracy," an elective and representative delegation whose basic unit is the friary. Only those points which will have been submitted in writing, based on a decision of the majority of brothers in a friary, will be brought before the chapter. The excesses of the ministers, custodians and guardians will be denounced in this way. The friars elect four definitors. They may correct the provincial and establish the chapter agenda with him, on points such as the division of custodies or the designation of lectors. One cannot be a definitor at two consecutive chapters. A fifth definitor will be elected in reserve, to enable the formation of a majority in case the four others are divided two against two in

---

[213] "Statuta generalia Ordinis," 301-04; "De fratrum minorum Constitutionibus praenarbonensibus," 74-75.

their assessment of the provincial, since supervision of the minister really constitutes the most important part of their task. Nothing will be submitted to the general chapter that has not received the assent of the majority of the provincial chapter.

With these four themes, the main points of the Order's government are sketched out. Let us add however that, in the rest of the document, it is specified that, as regards recruitment, only clerics having studied at the university (grammar, logic, medicine, canon or civil law, theology) with the notable exception of clerics and lay persons whose entrance would be a credit to the glory of the Order, may be received into the Order.[214] This is tactfully put, but it's a shutting out, all the same.

The first striking aspect in this group of clauses is the powerful influence of the *Constitutions* of the Friars Preacher on the later institutional development of the Minors;[215] in this, we perceive the influence of Haymo of Faversham. Also to be considered is to what extent all this effort, and therefore these borrowings, aim at preventing the recurrence of the misadventures of the last years of Elias's generalate. The basic principle, in a clearly "clericalized" Order, is the superiority of the general chapter over all the other authorities of the Order, since the assembly designates the minister general and deposes him without any possible recourse, while it establishes itself as the last appeal within the institution, including appeals against it own visitators. It is indeed significant that the visitators, who until then were the formidable cogs in the machine of the minister general, are henceforth defined as envoys of the chapter. Just as the case of a recalcitrant general facing the chapter is decided without hesitation, the obligatory

---

[214] *Ibid.*, 75.
[215] R. Brooke, *Early Franciscan Government ...*, 225-31 and 293-96.

minimal frequency for convoking chapters prevents the temptation that Elias had not resisted. The series of systematically distrustful measures concerning superiors, which finds its culmination in the severe examination to which the general is subjected as a prelude to the work of the chapter, and the proliferation of control procedures, sum up the spirit of a legislation intended to take into account the lessons of a recent past.

From the standpoint of deliberative and electoral processes, the 1239 clauses represent an extraordinary effort at precision in comparison with the vagueness of the *Later Rule*. In compliance with the law determined by the Fourth Lateran Council, the principle of absolute majority prevails in every situation. The ballots are organized, public, put down in writing, and announced as soon as possible. Everything is done to avoid dispute (the definitor in reserve to make a majority emerge) or to prevent moments of indecision (the periods of vacancy whose terms are provided for) with clearly defined provisional delegations. The deliberative processes appear even more respectful of a community basis than the elections, since the proposals for the agenda and for its content issue from the internal majority of a friary, then from the majority of a provincial chapter, before going back to the general chapter where they are considered and decided upon by the majority. We know that such a procedure, under the appearance of great openness, can also enable the expression of minorities – no matter how important they are – to be blocked, for their voice has no chance to overcome all the barriers of the majority. Therein lie the discreet charms of "democratic centralism..."

The system appears less carefully developed from the standpoint of the general structure and the channels of selection. This is in fact the consequence of a shrinking back from the community process, which must certainly not be held against the 1239 *Constitutions*, but to which the 1260 version testifies, to which we have had to refer to fill in the gaps of the original text. The ministers, at both the general and provincial levels, are elected by the chapters and are removable by them. Very good. But how are the chapters set up? The provincial assembly is in fact composed of one representative chosen from each friary and the custodians. But nothing tells us who designates the custodians – or the guardians, for that matter. We remember that Jordan of Giano lets it be understood that the election of guardians and custodians by the friars had been established by the preliminary committee at the 1239 general chapter, then confirmed by the general chapter itself and approved by the Sovereign Pontiff. We remember also that Thomas of Eccleston had told us that the statute had been abolished after the failure of the first – and, according to him the last – chapter specifically for definitors (in 1241). We must believe that this clause, indeed enacted but dropped some two or three years after its publication, was either in the parts missing from the Casanatense double leaf, or, already invalid at the moment of copying, was not kept by the scribe. Moreover, the same reasoning may be applied for the statute concerning the separate chapters of definitors, established in 1239 and abolished in 1242, by recalling that everything that dealt with general chapters and most of that which has to do with provincial chapters in the preceding account had, perforce, to be derived from the conditions of the statutes in 1260. Since the custodians ceased being elected themselves – the hypothesis can be made that this was in 1242 – the election of the provincial minister, like his potential deposing, is thus in fact greatly determined by the individuals appointed by his predecessor – indeed, by himself in the second case. On the other hand, it seems that the various friaries, whatever their size, all had a one and only one representative, therefore a one and only one voice. These two peculiarities (indifference to the numerical basis of representation and reversal of the original chain of appointments between provincial and custodian) has repercussions on the general chapter, since each province is represented there by the provincial minister, a custodian, and an elected representative of the chapter – that is to say, three individuals whose relationship with the rank-and-file of the brothers is, in one way or another, disconnected by this change in the selection of the custodians.

It's not a question of holding this breach of the democratic process against the Friars Minor of the early 1240s! Yet it's in the very light of the era's series of events – not of an *a priori* idea of "democratic progress" – that the questioning of a collective designation of guardians and custodians, which had nevertheless been established in 1239, seems like a stepping back, or, very precisely, a withdrawal. What exactly happened between 1239 and 1242, the probable date of the Bologna Chapter that followed that of the definitors at Montpellier?[216] It doesn't appear possible to reconstruct it in detail. Let us be content with successively citing and in this way leaving to the reader's imagination the accounts of Jordan of Giano, Thomas of Eccleston, and Brother Pellegrino of Bologna in 1305, himself taken up again by Arnold of Sarrant in the later *Chronicle of the XXIV Generals:*

> Thus, in the year of the Lord 1239, according to what had been said, the discreet friars, sent out from various provinces and flocking to Rome, ordered, by the opinion and the will of the Lord Pope and with the approbation of the general

---

[216] *Chronica XXIV generalium*, 247-48. R. Brooke, *Early Franciscan Government*, 235-46, rightly attaches great importance to the Bologna Chapter.

chapter, that the elections of ministers, custodians and guardians be done in a different way than that observed until then. Furthermore, they decided that each minister in his province would hold a chapter and his subordinates two.[217]

Now [to Brother Albert] succeeded Brother Haymo, an Englishman, who took great care to carry through what his predecessor had begun. Under his administration the first and last general chapter of definitors that ever occurred in the Order was held, because of their insolence of course, for they wished, by all possible means, to make all the ministers who were present at the chapter, as well as the minister general, leave from the place; and it was so. Also, the statute that had been made regarding this same chapter of subordinates in the presence of the pope at the moment of Brother Elias's deposing and also the one regarding the canonical election of guardians and custodians, because of this insolence of the subordinates, were abolished at the following general chapter. Certain brothers wished to completely eliminate the Order's custodians, saying that this office was unnecessary.[218]

The sixth [minister general] was Brother Haymo the Englishman, Doctor of Sacred Theology, who first went around the entire Order by visiting the provinces, despite his advanced age. He took great care in the celebration of the Divine Office. He also began to diminish the status and the power [*potentiam*] of the lay brothers, who until

---

[217] Jordan of Giano, *Chronica*, 65.
[218] Thomas of Eccleston, *De adventu*, 13.

then exercised managerial offices [*praelationis officia*].[219]

Another document throws some light on this period of time so fraught with major decisions. The one assembly of definitors was not totally without effect. Between May 13, 1241 and June 7, 1242, in response to the request of the Montpellier Chapter, four Friars Minor masters of the University of Paris – Alexander of Hales, John of La Rochelle, Robert of La Bassée and Odo Rigaldus – compose an "Exposition of the Rule" and address it, in company with the custodian of Paris Geoffrey of Brie, to the minister Haymo of Faversham and to the general chapter (of Bologna) on behalf of the province of France.[220]

Each province of the Order must have done the same,[221] but this one alone has come down to us. This is not exactly a mere coincidence. The presence of the complete text of the Four Masters in twenty-seven manuscripts (one from the thirteenth century, five from the fourteenth, sixteen from the fifteenth and five from the sixteenth) – not counting the fragments and the lost codices – and its seven printed editions that occur between 1502 and 1535 attest to its circulation, its enduring fame and its authority, just as does the reference that is continually made to it in the later *Commentaries*, with the sole exception of that of John of Wales. Unlike the papal letters or the *Constitutions* however, this text,

---

[219] Pellegrino of Bologna, *Chronicon abbreviatum*, 142; *Chronica XXIV generalium*, 251: "This general, Brother Haymo, decreed the lay brothers unfit for the Order's offices that, until then, they had fulfilled like clerics."

[220] *Ibid.*, 247-48. G.L. Potestà, "Maestri e dottrine nel XIII secolo," in *Francesco d'Assisi e il primo secolo di storia francescana*, 308-09.

[221] Thomas of Eccleston, *De adventu*, 13.

strictly speaking, is not normative, since it doesn't have the force of law and was not to be put into practice. But it must be integrated into this effort of the institution's reflection on the institution soon after – indeed, on the brink of – the crisis of 1239, because two of the masters who work on it – Alexander of Hales and John of La Rochelle – had participated some years earlier in the "savage" chapter against Elias.

Alexander of Hales is a native of England. Engaged at the University of Paris, he already has a Master of Arts in 1210. Before 1220, he is a master in the school of theology. In 1236, at a mature age, he enters the Order of Friars Minor, which causes quite a stir: such a learned person in an Order of ignoramuses! He transfers his chair of theology near to the Paris friary and takes over the running of the *studium*. Author of the first scholastic *Summa Theologica,* he has as disciples such minds as John of La Rochelle and Bonaventure. With the former, he participates in the resistance against Elias. He dies on August 21, 1245. John of La Rochelle receives a Masters of Arts and becomes master of theology at the University of Paris. He joins the Order of Friars Minor well before 1238, then works with Alexander of Hales, writing a good part of the *Summa* which bears the name of the English friar, exercises the office of assistant regent of the *studium* on the side and dies the same year as Alexander, on February 3, 1245. Besides his theological works, he was also a talented preacher, as his preserved sermons testify. Odo Rigaldus is younger. He enters the Order of Friars Minor in 1236 and his contribution to the *Exposition of the Rule* seems to be one of his first collaborations with his two elders. He becomes regent master of the *studium* in February 1245, and master of theology in 1246. His selection as Archbishop of Rouen on March 5, 1247 firmly alters the course of his existence. The prelate, haughty about his rights, becomes very close to Louis

IX, devotes himself to diplomacy and brings back the remains of his deceased royal friend in 1270, before passing away himself on July 2, 1275. Of Robert of La Bassée, native of Flanders, very few things are known, apart from his affiliation with the University of Paris and his participation in the "Exposition of the Rule."

What is clear is that the province of France has placed itself completely in the hands of a university staff, relegating to obscurity even Custodian Geoffrey of Brie whom tradition does not hold among the authors of the commissioned text. We are far from the response that Francis, at a time when such a commentary was demanded by the Minors of the English province, is supposed to have given, according to Thomas of Eccleston, in a dream to Brother John of Bannister:

> My son, go find the lay brothers and they will explain the *Rule* to you![222]

The commentary that the Four Masters give to Chapter VIII of the *Later Rule* – the "constitutional" chapter *par excellence*, which will now hold our attention in the many texts to be studied – revolves around the relationship of precedence between general chapter and minister general, which is not surprising.[223] If the friars (the definitors, that is), the minister general and the provincials took measures in chapter "regarding the limitation of the power [*de coarctatione potestatis*] of the minister general," or defining the form of chapters and elections, can the minister general modify them in the name of the obedience which the friars owe him

---

[222] Id., *ibid.*, 13.

[223] *Expositio quatuor magistrorum super Regulam fratrum minorum (1241-1242)*, ed. L. Oliger (Rome, 1950), 160-62.

according to the very terms of the *Rule*? The Four Masters respond: the *Rule* provides that chapters be held and that their decisions, which legitimately aim at "keeping the perfection and purity of the religion" and saving it from any danger, constrain the minister general. He cannot invalidate them, even when they are the very ones that would limit the minister's powers. Neither the superiors alone nor the friars alone can change the ordinances made communally in general chapter and approved by the pope.

This brief passage is full of lessons. Hammered out here, as was probably the case in the barely studied *Constitutions,* is the superiority of the chapter over the minister general, but the argument is not immaterial. The source of all legitimacy in the Order is the *Rule,* "which prevails in authority over the general chapter," the external guarantee being that of papal approval. The authority of the chapter ensues from the *auctoritas* of the *Rule,* which in the Latin lexicon contrasts with the *potestas* of the ministers; it is an argumentation, we note, against which may be naturally put forward the first lines of Chapter VIII of the *Later Rule* itself, which precede the evocation of the "Pentecost chapter:"

> Let all the brothers be bound always to have one of the brothers of this religion as minister general and servant of the entire brotherhood, and let them be firmly bound to obey him.[224]

Chronologically, in the founding statutory text, the superior precedes the assembly. The institutional vision of the Four Masters, in the form of a cascade of legitimacy – *Rule*, chapter, minister –, under obviously serene appearances, expresses a very diplomatic choice.

---

[224] LR 8:1.

Another argument, of the contractual type, is added to this authority-based conception: the decisions of the chapter are the outcome of the mingled wills of superiors and inferiors, which neither of the two parties may put into question again in a unilateral way. This is not to say in any way that there would be a source of legitimacy in the body of the community – very much on the contrary, since superiors and inferiors are conceived of as two independent entities, who together must come up with an agreement that can be assumed to take the form of a compromise. It is to be definitively confirmed that the one general chapter gathers the superiors and the envoys of the subordinates.

The following question focuses on the passage from Chapter VIII that provides for the deposing of an unfit minister general and his replacement by means of new elections. The general's inadequacies must be recognized, specifies the *Rule*, by all (*universitas*) of the provincial ministers and custodians. The Masters ask themselves:

> What does *universitas* mean? According to the law, *universitas* means the majority [*maior pars*].

The "law" here is obviously, once again, Canon 24 of the Fourth Lateran Council. The Masters note next that the term "custodian" is confused in the *Rule* with that of "minister" – general or not – and that the term "guardian" does not appear there at all. Pointing out that some infer from this that the *Rule* does not require obedience to guardians, to resolve the dilemma, our authors propose to stop using this term and to substitute for it that of "custodians or ministers of the house." This proposal was almost certainly debated at the Bologna Chapter, hence the distorted rumor, hawked by Thomas of Eccleston, according to which some would have wanted to eliminate the custodians. A trivial matter, it may be said, but revealing: our authors cleverly dispose of the real underlying question – that of the mode of the guardians' selection – and, pretending to see in the debate only a matter of vocabulary, they base their response on the necessary correspondence between the legitimate literalness of the *Rule* and the authorities of power in the Order.

In the final analysis, the "Exposition of the Four Masters" proves to us that, contrary to what we might tend to believe, there was not one response to the crisis of 1239, but a range of possible responses, unless there was another rapid evolution of the same individuals' positions in the past. In 1241-1242, the positions of these Parisian academics, certainly more theologians than jurists, seems very different from what may be reconstructed from the 1239 *Constitutions* and perhaps comes to shed a little light on the reasons for the dissatisfaction people had with them, probably in 1242. A collective structure of power in the Order, as it were out of nothing, is opposed – or succeeded – by a scholastic elaboration where the authority can come only from the text, but where the founding text is interpreted in the sense that suits the authors, representatives of the university elite. Their real premise is the joint presence of two previous categories in the Order: superiors and subordinates. No doubt that Haymo of Faversham understood the message perfectly. More generally, what issues from this question about the concept of *universitas* is that the affirmation of the majority principle is perhaps a necessary, but in no way a sufficient, condition of a "democratic" conception of the institution.

The deliberations of the Bologna General Chapter could not once again get papal approval. And for a good reason: The Roman See remains vacant from November 10, 1241 to June 25, 1243. From Lyons where he held council, on November 14, 1245, the new pontiff,

Sinibaldo Fieschi-become-Innocent IV (1243-1254), addresses to the entire Order of Friars Minors the letter *Ordinem vestrum*.[225] The missive proposes to resolve "the few doubts and obscure passages" of the *Rule*, as had previously been done by Gregory IX in the *Quo elongati*. Thus, fifteen years later, we have the second papal commentary on the *Later Rule*. The only passage that dealt with the basic operation of the institution is a repeat of the 1230 letter: a single custodian will represent the group of custodians from a province. As for the rest, the Order is henceforth firmly set up in the fiction of the "poor use" of its goods, whose ownership is assumed by the Roman See.

It is remarkable that Innocent IV, a solid canonist, did not think he should reaffirm the position of the papacy on the institutional debates that had been troubling the Order since the deposition of Elias. Does that mean that the 1239 clauses, revised and corrected in 1242, had his tacit agreement? Nevertheless, the entire pronouncement of the *Ordinem vestrum,* including its repetitions of *Quo elongati*, is careful to bring to the fore the friar priests and the provincial ministers who share most of the prerogatives of the general, while the role of the chapter is not at all emphasized. The Apostolic See, always playing the superiors' card, may, depending on unknown factors, hesitate between two strategies: rely on the minister general, or lean on the caste of provincial ministers.

But strategy is not enough. The friars – some of them anyway – must have taken offense at a papal letter that barely recognized the spiritual specificity of their Order. Thomas of Eccleston tells us that they decided, in general chapter (that of Genoa in 1251, or of Metz in 1254), to suspend the interpretation of the *Rule* by Innocent IV,

---

[225] *Bullarium franciscanum...*, 1, 400-02.

judged to be too lax, in preference for that of Gregory IX.[226]

Around 1252, according to David Flood,[227] the Provençal brother Hugh of Digne composes in his turn a *Rule Commentary*, in obedience to a given order, he says. By whom? No one knows. Moreover, we know very little about the life of this author, who nevertheless had a very great reputation. A Friar Minor, his influence spreads between Southern France and Northern Italy in the second quarter of the thirteenth century and he once holds the office of Provincial Minister of Provence. More well-known is his sister Douceline, who lives as a recluse in Hyères, then in Marseilles, where she dies on September 1, 1274. Without ties to the University of Paris, Hugh is nevertheless very cultured: "one of the greatest clerics in the world, an eminent preacher and greatly loved by the clergy and by the people, excellent in debate and competent in all things."[228] On July 17, 1254, he preaches before Louis IX upon his return from the Crusades, producing an intense emotion in the Monarch that is said to have greatly impacted the second part of his reign. He dies between 1254 and 1257. Three Latin treatises of Hugh of Digne have been preserved: two focusing on poverty and our *Commentary*. Was he "the great Joachimite" whose portrait Salimbene enthusiastically paints?[229] There is a tendency today to put the import of this testimony into perspective.

To fittingly comment on the *Rule*, which too many brothers do not know or know without living it, Hugh went to question the surviving companions of Francis,

---

[226] Thomas of Eccleston, *De adventu*, 9.

[227] D. Flood, *Hugh of Digne's Rule Commentary*, Spicilegium bonaventurianum, 14 (Grottaferrata, 1979), 50-54.

[228] Salimbene, *Cronica*, 324.

[229] Id., *ibid.*, 339.

brothers renowned for their sanctity.[230] To know, understand and live the *Rule* daily in that mid-century as in the days of the founder: such seems to be the goal of the undertaking. Our author also attentively read the *Commentary on the Rule of Saint Augustine* of Hugh of St. Victor, the *Dialogues* of Gregory the Great and the *De praecepto et dispensatione* of Bernard of Clairvaux. He is thoroughly familiar with the *Exposition* of the Four Paris Masters.[231] His work will nevertheless not achieve the fame of his predecessors' work; besides a fifteenth-century manuscript, the only parts of it that remain are five editions, dating from 1506 to 1513, and the manuscript of an Italian translation dating to 1503.

In his commentary of Chapter VIII,[232] Hugh of Digne successively cites the *Later Rule* and the Four Masters. But on the relationships between minister general and chapter, he does so to distinguish himself from his predecessors. Indeed, he puts forward the opinion of some who indicate that the general should be obeyed in all circumstances, provided that he doesn't question the purity of the *Rule*, which the chapter guarantees. It is to the minister that the *Rule* requires the brothers pledge obedience (and we cannot help noting that the first lines of Chapter VIII of the *Later Rule*, neglected by the Four Masters, confirm here the opinion expounded by Hugh of Digne).[233] He is head of the chapter and of the Order, and it is not for the subjects to judge the decisions of the superior. At this moment, there is the feeling that the author has become a partisan of the viewpoint that, in

---

[230] Hugh of Digne, *Expositio super Regulam fratrum minorum*, ed. D. Flood, *Hugh of Digne's Rule Commentary*, 91-92.

[231] A. Sisto, *Figure del primo francescanesimo in Provenza: Ugo e Douceline di Digne*, Biblioteca della Rivista di storia e letteratura religiosa, Studi e Testi, 3 (Florence, 1971), 103-14.

[232] Hugh of Digne, *Expositio*, 172-75.

[233] LR 8:2.

the beginning, he seemed to be content with reporting. The *Rule*, he adds, nevertheless grants to the chapter the power, and even the duty, to depose the minister who would demonstrate his inadequacy.

In the event of the general's death, it is not advisable to immediately convoke a special chapter; rather, it is necessary to wait for the following Pentecost chapter to hold the election of his successor. This is a measure in keeping with the letter of the *Rule*, probably provided for by the *Constitutions* of 1239 and in any case recorded, with more detail, in those of 1260. Since provincial ministers and custodians are explicitly mentioned as the ones considering holding the election or the deposaing of the minister, it is obvious, concludes Hugh, that the custodians are a part of the general chapter in the same way as the provincials. Nothing is said here of the discreet friars, of which the *Rule* actually makes no mention, but it may be wondered whether Hugh militates in this way for the integration of the custodians into the definitors. All the provincials must be present at the chapter; for the custodians, the provisions of the *Quo elongati* prevail. The absolute majority suffices to depose the minister general, as well as to elect him, without the necessity of a two-thirds majority.

Hugh of Digne doesn't attach excessive importance to the fluctuations of terms between minister general, provincials, custodians and guardians, which, for all that, do not make the duties change. But he does mention that, formerly, the guardians were appointed by the custodians, who were named by the provincials, who were themselves appointed by the general. Yet he does not reconsider the current mode of appointing guardians. Does this mean that he prefers the old one? He finally affirms that three types of chapters were required by the *Rule* – at the Order, province, and custody levels.

Regarding the conventual chapter, there is no obligation to convoke it regularly.

Without a doubt, in the face of the 1239 *Constitutions* as well as the *Exposition of the Four Masters*, Hugh of Digne's text represents a return to a conception that is clearly more favorable to the minister general in the distribution of powers within the Order. But the cleverness of the Provençal – Salimbene calls it formidable – is to pose the question not in terms of power, but authority[234] – paternal authority, in fact:

> The saint, lover of unity, wished to equip his family with a single head [*caput*] and that one man be the shepherd of his entire herd.[235]

Armed with this eminently evangelical vocabulary, it is a family – almost patriarchal – vision of the Order that is again proposed here, with a frequent legitimating reference to the "ancient" times of the beginnings. Undoubtedly this is the way Hugh of Digne would respond to the wishes of the minister general, his good friend John of Parma (1247-1257). This spiritual brother, anxious to revive the strictness of the observance by recourse to the original teachings of Francis, is above all else a paternal and pastoral figure and, beyond his forced resignation of 1257 and his condemnation of 1263, he will be remembered as "the patriarch of Greccio." Furthermore, around 1252, as Hugh is writing, he can reasonably say to himself that time has passed since Elias's deposition. The danger of autocracy seems averted and the figure of a minister general possessing a certain reflection of the founder's charisma can resurface. It is

---

[234] Hugh of Digne, *Expositio*, 176, regarding who grants the office of preaching.

[235] Id., *ibid.*, 172.

a way of claiming the specificity of being a Minor as a Franciscan specificity. It is thus also – not word for word, but in spirit – an indirect response to the *Ordinem vestrum*.

From 1239 to the early 1250's, to fill the great gap in institutional matters left wide open by the founder's original negligence and by multiple roadblocks of Elias's generalate, there was then a flowering of discussions and gestations, of interventions internal or external to the Order of Friars Minor, to define in the most exact way the manner in which this large body was to be governed. The discussion was so lively and so prolific that in 1254, at the Metz General Chapter, the minister John of Parma, by Salimbene's account, thought to call for a moratorium in his reply to the ministers and custodians who were asking for a new legislative effort:

> Let us not create more constitutions, but rather observe well those that we have![236]

With that, Hugh of Digne's labor may seem to have fizzled out. He nevertheless points out a reorientation that was not to remain short-lived. The almost final resolution of the equation, not as far removed from John of Parma's order as it might seem to be, comes with the great legislative work of Bonaventure contained in the *Constitutions* enacted on June 10, 1260 by the Narbonne General Chapter called together under his authority.

John of Fidanza, who later takes the name of Bonaventure, is born around 1221 in Bagnoregio, near Viterbo. In 1235, he goes to Paris, where he begins his studies and, in 1243, is awarded a Master of Arts degree. He is then received into the Order of Friars Minor and undertakes theological studies at the Paris *studium*. After

---

[236] Salimbene, *Cronica*, 438.

having carried out the now mandatory commentary on Peter Lombard's *Book of Sentences*, he receives, from the hands of John of Parma in 1253, license to teach theology. Promoted to regent master of the *studium*, he defends the Order in the dispute against William of Saint Amour and the secular masters. Illustrating the vocation of the Friar Minor without ever falling into Joachimite interpretations, Bonaventure finds himself in fundamental agreement with a pope, Alexander IV (1254-1261), who condemns in turn the arguments of Friar Minor Gerardo of Borgo San Donnino, extrapolations of the works of the Calabrian Abbot, in 1255, and then attacks of William of Saint Amour in 1256.

The same pontiff persuades John of Parma to resign at the February, 1257 chapter and, in the February 2 session over which he personally presides, he sees Bonaventure elected Minister General, an office which the latter will hold until May 20, 1273. On April 23, 1257, the new minister sends from Paris, and not from Rome where the chapter had met but from which he was absent, a circular letter to all the provincials, the *Licet insufficientiam meam*. In it, he develops a veritable program of reform, denouncing the ten recurring errors that endanger the Order and systematically setting the content of the *Later Rule* against them.

In fact, the design of the *Constitutions* of Narbonne was already set in its broad outline. Other statutes of the same type, as will be remembered, had been composed before 1260 – those of the 1239 chapter in particular. But it is not surprising that for a long time they had escaped scholarly investigation and had only been brought to light recently, thanks to the meticulousness of Cesar Cenci. This is indeed understandable from the viewpoint of the *Statutes* of the same Narbonne Chapter, which record the assembly's current decisions and which, after having ordered each guardian to keep the

General Constitutions in his friary – to not communicate it outside but to have it read during meals, especially the first seven chapters – provides:

> And once these [the *Constitutions* of Narbonne] are enacted, let the old ones be destroyed.[237]

It must therefore be understood that the 1260 chapter, which integrated into its *Constitutions* a part of the previous writings and which, as Salimbene asserts and as the discovery of the Casanatense double leaf proves, mainly repeated most of the decisions of 1239, did not hope to be able to trace the course of this progressive historical construction. It is difficult to miss the striking parallel with the composition of the *Statutes* of the 1266 Paris Chapter, which provides for the destruction of all legends of Francis previous to those written by Bonaventure.[238] The parallel doesn't end there. If it is not necessary to refrain, as we had done after Luigi Pellegrini, from reconstructing the missing parts of the 1239 text with the help of that of 1260, we should also point out, – in the passages that deal with the same subjects and are preserved in the two versions, and by the general layout of the rubrics, the drafting of each article, the additions and omissions – the way in which Bonaventure succeeded in doing that at which he excels: bringing something new from the old.

It would remain, further down the line, to do a similar collation with the revisions of the statutes produced, among others, by the Assisi General Chapter in 1279 and that of Paris in 1292. The 1260 text is preserved for us in

---

[237] "'Diffinitiones' capituli generalis o.f.m. narbonensis (1260)," ed. F.M. Delorme, *Archivum franciscanum historicum*, 3 (1910): 502.

[238] "Definitiones capitulorum generalium Ordinis fratrum minorum, 1260-1282," ed. A.G. Little, *Archivum franciscanum historicum*, 7 (1914): 678.

a single manuscript, which moreover resurfaces only in the early sixteenth century. The Assisi and Paris drafts are respectively represented by six and three copies; it's a peculiarity of this normative literature that the old state is absorbed by the subsequent ones, with or without a standing order to destroy them. Let us be content for the moment with skimming through the 1260 text, favoring the points that are newly clarified in comparison to the earlier version.

While the double leaf containing the 1239 text lacks a beginning, the *Constitutions* of Narbonne are equipped with a *Prologue*, most certainly attributable to Bonaventure personally. The opportunity is nevertheless taken to present this labor as the work of the general chapter. It is the means of reminding us that making legislation truly comes within its remit, since "with it lies the highest governmental authority of the Order" [*precipua residet auctoritas Ordinis gubernandi*].[239] We recognize here the opinion of the Paris Masters who, on this point, were certainly in agreement with the 1239 text. The minister general is forbidden to make "a general statute, other than in general chapter, with the assent of the definitors";[240] as regards the provincial ministers, they must be on guard against the proliferation of constitutions peculiar to a province.[241]

While the Order now has a variety of sharply contrasting statutes and offices which take it a long way from the permutability of functions according to the *Rule For Hermitages* (ministers, custodians, guardians,

---

[239] "Statuta generalia Ordinis," 38.
[240] *Ibid.*, 86. Certain additions from the 1292 Paris Chapter, *ibid.*, 41, 52-53 and 68, nevertheless prove the determining role of the minister general in the development of legislation.
[241] *Ibid.*, 87.

lectors, confessors, preachers and procurators)[242] and while the barriers between lay brothers and priests are more and more impenetrable (and let no one rise from the lay to the clerical state without the license of the general)[243], the unity of the whole is nevertheless asserted in the most immediately visible way: by the habit, which must be strictly the same for all, "without distinction."[244] In every facet of daily life, within the Order as well as in contact with the outside, nothing concerning the measures most material to intellectual exercise may be done without the express permission of superiors, out of strict respect for the hierarchical order. Corrections, measured but firm, are provided for – far more numerous in the Narbonne version than in its predecessor, as Salimbene anticipates;[245] it is not within the superiors' remit to change the penalties or to absolve them.[246] Regarding denunciation by the visitators in general chapter of superiors guilty of living in high style or of leading a life of idleness:[247] their deposings are very much provided for, but the grounds for such a decision must be voiced abroad as little as possible.[248]

Sections VIII to XI are those that most directly concern power – its exercise and control in the Order. The section dealing with "province visits" is almost a repetition of the 1239 text.[249] The section dealing with "elections

---

[242] *Ibid.*, 42. The brothers adorned here with the title of "procurators" are those who represent the Order's interests to the Apostolic See and should not to be confused with the lay procurators who manage the friaries' goods; Gratien de Paris, *Histoire de la fondation* ..., 183-88; Marinus a Neukirchen, *De capitulo generali* ..., 148-49.

[243] "Statuta generalia Ordinis," 71.

[244] *Ibid.*, 42-3.

[245] In particular *ibid.*, 82-7.

[246] *Ibid.*, 86.

[247] *Ibid.*, 65 and 69.

[248] *Ibid.*, 84.

[249] *Ibid.*, 284-288.

of ministers" is almost a word for word repetition concerning minister generals and provincials. But added to this, in the 1260 version, are the necessary details regarding the designation of custodians and guardians which – an accident of preservation or a consequence already of the calamitous Montpellier Chapter – are missing in the Casanatense double leaf. It is again very much the provincial minister's responsibility to appoint custodians in provincial chapter, with the counsel of the definitors and the brothers of the custody present. If a custodian dies or is deposed before the provincial chapter, the provincial minister will be able to provide for his replacement merely with the counsel of the six "discreet" friars of the concerned custody. Guardians are appointed in exactly the same way, with an additional recommendation from the area custodian, but without systematic consultation with the brothers of the friary. Whether the vacancy of the guardian's post occurs through death or through the deposing of the incumbent, the counsel of a few discreet friars from the area will be recorded all the same. A friary is defined as the place where twelve or more brothers live. The non-conventual guardians may be appointed directly by the custodian.[250] At all levels of the hierarchy, there is no mention of a term for the superiors' offices, which must therefore be a lifetime one, subject to deposing.

In the Casanatense double leaf, the section dealing with "the provincial chapter" gets the smallest share and that dealing with "the general chapter" is totally absent. Hence, we have summarized its terms above on the basis

---

[250] *Ibid.*, 294-95. It is the 1292 Paris Chapter which will recognize that they must be regarded "as superiors [*pro praelatis*];" the minimum age for all superiors will be fixed at thirty years; *ibid.*, 298 and 300.

of the Narbonne text, all collation between the 1239 draft and that of 1260 being physically impossible here.

All things considered, the legislative labor of Bonaventure, who we sometimes like to honor with the title of "second founder of the Order of Friars Minor," must be neither exaggerated nor underestimated. The *Constitutions* of Narbonne do not break new ground, strictly speaking, but they are essential as the remarkable synthesis of twenty years of reflection on the institution's governance. They furnish the conclusion of the scheme that we have been following from its beginning.

In summary and to return to the simple but pertinent observation post of the relationship between ministers and chapters, the role of the general chapter is greatly exalted. This can be seen from the very fact that these *Constitutions* are products of a general chapter, from the fact that it is recognized as "the superior governmental authority of the Order," from the fact that the visitators are its agents, and from the fact that it has adopted a double role – and this almost certainly since 1242 – based on a structure characteristic of the Order of Friars Preachers: the separate chapters of priors and definitors. With the Minors, the control by the province's elected members, the "discreet" friars, is no longer practiced outside the superiors' assembly but within it, provincials and discreets sharing in the performance of the definitors' function, which, without a doubt, greatly reduces its critical impact.

While the theoretical surveillance of the ministers by the friars remains unchanged, the many directives encouraging absolute discretion about these matters do not allow for the slightest discussion. Above all, the permanent necessity of requiring friars to obtain permission from the superior to engage in studies places the superiors in the position of defining the orthodoxy of the doctrine proclaimed in the Order. This caste puts real power in the hands of university-trained priests increased by the exercise of these functions which includes levying required penalties for theological error. Their discretionary power in the recommendations of prospective custodians also allows them to have a strong influence on the composition of chapters. While nominally under the authority of the minister general, it is indeed up to "our masters" to determine the correctness of the opinions put forward by the friars.[251] In addition, the clause of the 1239 *Constitutions* limiting recruitment in the Order to clerics armed with a university education, and the measure brought back by Pellegrino of Bologna and Arnold of Sarrant which, beginning with Haymo of Faversham's generalate, excluded the remaining lay brothers from holding superiors' offices, and thus, the tasks assigned to the latter remarkably reduce, *ipso facto*, the job profile.

To return to the beginning, if the legislating function in the Order is theoretically passed on to the general chapter, the very fact that everyone, beginning with Salimbene, agrees to acknowledge the *Constitutions* of Narbonne as Bonaventure's work speaks volumes on the weight of the "executive" at the very core of the "legislative!"

The subtle embroidery of the text, where all the threads woven since 1239 in the process of the institution's reflection on the institution are found, can only be admired. The community construction of the 1239 *Constitutions* forms, on the surface, the backdrop of the 1260 text. But from 1242 onwards, it had been in part emptied of its substance. The reference to a legitimacy coming from the rank and file, which comes out in the 1239 clauses, had been damaged, among other things, by the *Exposition* of the Four Masters. The

---

[251] *Ibid.*, 73. D. Flood, *The Order's Masters*, 56-68.

Exposition, which made all legitimacy ensue from the *Rule*, certainly asserted the authority of the chapter against the power of the ministers, but established the latter for doing this in a category completely separate from subordinates, without a link between them from cause to effect. These two elements coming from the Parisian university – the definite authority of the chapter and again, the self-sufficiency of the ministers – are present in the 1260 *Constitutions*, since they had probably already had an influence on the measures taken under Haymo of Faversham's generalate. Hugh of Digne had attempted to return – for want of having charismatic minister generals – to the model of a patriarchal figure as minister general. He thus opposed, discreetly, the Four Masters. Already, the convergences between the *Letter in Response to Three Questions of an Unknown Master* composed by Bonaventure in 1254-1255 and the *Commentary* of Hugh of Digne were obvious.[252] Again, in the *Constitutions* of Narbonne, a fundamental closeness between the Provençal brother and the minister general asserts itself around the importance of the pastoral figure of the minister himself. His leadership role was explicitly advanced by Hugh of Digne. It is even more striking that this viewpoint is not so clearly expressed in the 1260 *Constitutions*, which doesn't mean – very much to the contrary – that it was not implicitly very present there.

We could stop here, for the line of this question which we are attempting to follow from its premises finds its resolution for the most part in the Bonaventurian legislation. However, so as not to disregard six texts that pertain fully to the typology of the *Rule* commentaries,

---

[252] R. Lambertini, *Apologia e crescita dell'identità francescana (1255-1279)*, Nuovi Studi storici, 4 (Rome, 1990), 43-64; L. Pellegrini, *art. cit.*, 17-22.

but without claiming in any way to account for the events that arise from 1260 to the 1320's in and around the Order of Friars Minor, we will proceed to read quickly through the *Commentaries* of David of Augsburg, John Peckham, John of Wales, Nicholas III, Peter John Olivi and Angelo Clareno.

David of Augsburg, who possibly studied at Magdeburg, was novice master at Ratisbonne around the years 1235-1250 and, in 1246, is given the responsibility of conducting the canonical visitation of the city's canonesses. He dies on November 19, 1272, leaving numerous treatises in German. A Latin manuscript from Munich preserves his *Rule Commentary*, written in the last years of his life and in which may be perceived all the teaching experience of the former novice master.

The prologue begins with the words "the holy father Francis." This is a sign. God not only showed the saint how he was to live, but also how he was to lead others, by his example, toward a form of life modeled on the Gospel. The sanctity of the Friars Minor, canonized or not, is proof of the excellence of this way. The twelve chapters of the *Rule* are in imitation of the twelve apostles and the twelve gates of Jerusalem. Thus, it is understood, the Order prefigures the Church Militant and Triumphant. An historical reminder follows, unusual in this genre of literature and almost certainly done to suit its educational aims. The Order was founded in 1209, approved by Innocent III who granted it its *Rule*, which, after a few modifications, was officially recognized and registered by Honorius III. David announces that, just as he intended to do with regard to the ministers – general or provincial –, he will rely on the declarations of Gregory [IX] and Innocent [IV], on the *General Constitutions*, and on the tradition of Francis's former contemporaries. He warns us that he skips Honorius III's prologue, like he usually did, he says, "for the lay brothers and the novices."[253]

Moreover, for the first time, Chapter VIII of the *Rule* is commented on line by line: we are in full interlinear gloss, and too bad for the *Testament*! The obedience due the minister general is emphasized with particular insistence: whoever eludes it excludes himself from the Order. For the election of the aforementioned minister, it is specified that he must be chosen within the Order and that "there is to be no submitting of applications [*non postulatio est*]." The author adds that the chapter may be called together by the general at other times than the usual ones, but "with the assent of the chapter." The procedure for deposing the general is then detailed, just as is the meeting of the provincial chapters, without significant addition.[254]

Upon reading David of Augsburg's *Commentary*, we have the feeling of being for the first time in the presence of a non-problematic text. Certainly the purpose of the message explains much of this characteristic. The lay brothers and the novices, the preferred audience of our author, needed above all to obey, and at best to know the broad outlines of the institution's governance, but they have no need to be introduced to all the discussions in progress. However, it may also be assumed that ten or so years after the resolution introduced by the *General Constitutions* of Narbonne, the debate simply had no *raison d'être*. By his silence, the former novice master from Ratisbonne confirms the validity of the 1260 constitutions.

---

[253] *Expositio Regulae edita a frate David sanctissimo*, ed. E. Lempp, "David von Augsburg. Schriften aus der Handschrift der München-er Hof- und Staatsbibliothek Cod. lat. 15312 zum erstenmal veröffentlich," *Zeitschrift für Kirchengeschichte*, 19 (1899): 345-346.

[254] Id., *ibid.*, 358-59.

A new *Commentary* of the *Rule* of the Friars Minor, attributed to Bonaventure beginning in the fifteenth century, intended to restore luster to his reputation, was in fact written by John Peckham following the style of strict scholastic canons. The English cleric, after being educated at Paris and Oxford where he receives a Master of Arts degree, enters the Order around 1250-1255 at the town's Minor friary, within which he has the feeling of at last finding true wisdom. Pursuing his theological studies in Paris, he begins teaching there in 1269 and is appointed regent of the *studium* in the early 1270's. He then returns to teach at Oxford, is elected provincial minister of England in 1274 and assigned as master of the Sacred Palace at Rome in 1277, before being promoted to Archbishop of Canterbury on January 25, 1279. He dies on December 8, 1292. Involved from 1256 in the defense of the Order against the secular masters, he composes – probably in his Roman phase, from 1277 to 1279 – the text that most directly interests us.

The commentary of Chapter VIII of the *Later Rule* focuses first on the minister general who must demonstrate "authority" and "humility" and who guarantees "unity," "because without a leader, no *respublica* can be run very well; it is why the Lord gave importance to one apostle over the others." This is nothing like the teaching of the Four Masters, distant predecessors of John Peckham at the head of the Paris *studium*, who acknowledged only the minister's "power" and placed the "authority" in the hands of the general chapter. Here, the latter is simply compared to the gathering of the apostles receiving the Spirit, in clear reference to the time of Pentecost; there is no further detail on its operation.[255]

---

[255] John Peckham, published under Bonaventure's name, *Expositio super Regulam fratrum minorum*, in Bonaventure, *Opera omnia*, 8 (Quaracchi, 1898), 426-27.

Returning in his commentary on Chapter X about the humility of the ministers, John Peckham emphasizes that this virtue, a necessity for superiors, is in no way to influence the attitudes of subordinates; let the greatest act as if he were the least, very good – but let the least not dare to play at being the greatest! And if it is true that ministers are to be servants, servanthood is clarified, just as David of Augsburg did, as concerned "principally in what is useful for the salvation of souls."[256] If a parallel is established between these watered-down descriptions and those of the hierarchy found in the commentary of Chapter IX, based on the model of pseudo-dionysian hierarchies,[257] – of the Church, of course, though one cannot help thinking that the metaphor applies to the Order – it is understandable that, regarding their authority, the superiors have nothing to fear from the master of the Sacred Palace!

It is not a coincidence that this text was attributed to Bonaventure; we can imagine that the commentator of the 1270's says out loud what the minister general was thinking to himself. It can also be assumed, even if an author like John Peckham presents a positive illustration of the life according to Francis and not its tense defense, that the recurring attacks of the secular masters against the Friars Minor had the effect of tightening the ranks of the Order around its values and its hierarchy – a situation from which the entire long generalate of Bonaventure benefits. In fact, skipping over the *Constitutions* of Narbonne, themselves formally respectful of the statutes of 1239, John Peckham is, in some respects, in the tradition of the *Commentary* of Hugh of Digne. Totally reversing the position in comparison with the Four

---

[256] Id., *ibid.*, 432.
[257] Id., *ibid.*, 428.

Masters, the English friar exalts the founding authority of the minister general, the central figure of a hierarchical cascade where the seat of power is obvious – that is, at the top.

John of Wales composes his *Commentary on the Rule* at approximately the same time. Our Welshman, already possessing a Master of Arts degree and a Bachelor's degree in Theology from Oxford, enters the Order of Friars Minor, obtains his doctorate, then becomes the sixth lector of the Oxford friary around 1257-1258. From 1281 to 1283, he is regent of the Paris *studium*. In 1282, he is a member of the committee responsible for examining the works of Peter John Olivi. The date of his death is not known. His works, which for the most part are compilations for the use of preachers and students, enjoyed a great reputation and, consequently, a considerable circulation.

His *Commentary on the Rule*, which is known to us through a Latin edition from Venice dated from 1513, is conceived of in the same spirit – of formation and edification – and prefers the authentically Franciscan spiritual values–poverty, humility, a pilgrim's detachment, brotherhood and service, prayer and devotion – to the legal approaches of the statutory text. If one makes use of a rule for building houses, shouldn't the brothers take just as much advantage of the *Rule*, work of a founder which the author likes to call "inspired," to construct their spiritual edifice? Since this written work of John of Wales has not been published earlier, we give here below the translation of the entire commentary of Chapter VIII:

> Regarding the election of the minister general and the chapter of Pentecost:
> *Let all the brothers ... one of the brothers.* And in that lies a great capacity for organization [*ordinabilitas*] in the government of the Order;

indeed, in every *respublica*, so that it be governed with order, it is important that there be only one superior and ruler,[258] according to the words of Jerome (ep. 76)[259]: "only one emperor, only one judge per province, in a ship only one pilot, in the house only one master; in an army, no matter how large, one watches only one general. Again, for the same reason, when Rome was founded, it could not have two brothers as kings." And he takes examples from the beasts, saying, "animals, deprived of speech, and herds of wild beasts follow their guides. Among bees there are queens. Cranes follow one among them in a pattern that forms a letter." Blessed Francis, inspired, therefore instituted that there be only one minister general leading the Order, whom all *are bound to obey*. And so it was with the people of God in the beginning, for only one at a time was made sovereign pontiff like Aaron (Dt. 8)[260] and likewise for his successors. And he instituted that there be one common election of the minister, so that the one chosen be more easily accepted by all. He is indeed better accepted by all who is elected by all of one accord. And so that there be no flaw in the government, *let the brothers be bound to elect from themselves another as custodian* if some inadequacy had manifested itself on the part of the previous one; this is the equity of justice. As a result also of the fact that the brothers *are bound to meet* in general chapter, the unanimity of the Order is preserved; that leads to a great security.

---

[258] We recognize here an argument already put forward by John Peckham.

[259] Jerome, *Epistula* 125:15, in Saint Jerome, *Letters,* 7, ed. J. Labourt (Paris, 1961), 126-27.

[260] Cf. Ex 29: 29-30; 35:19; Lv 8 and 21.

That, indeed, is why they must meet: so that the state of the Order is preserved in its perfection; in return, they are consulted on the decisions to make, for "security lies in many counselors (Prv 24);"[261] this is why the Lord ordered Moses also to summon frequently the elders in council (Nm 11)[262] – "Assemble for me seventy of the elders of Israel."[263]

There, again, is the exalting of the superior with the backing of an inspired founder: a single and natural leader who seeks consensus, around whom the Order tightens its ranks.

For a third time, the Franciscan *Rule* is the object of a papal commentary with the constitution *Exiit qui seminat*, issued from Soriano by Nicholas III (1277-1280) on August 14, 1279. Giovanni Orsini is born into a noble Roman family that regularly cultivated devotion to Francis and his sons. Created Cardinal Deacon of Saint Nicholas in Carcere by Innocent IV in 1244, he becomes, under Urban IV (1261-1264), official protector of the Friars Minor in 1263. Elected pope, he confirms his affection for the male and female mendicant Orders, appointing several Minors to the head of bishoprics or integrating them into the Sacred College of Cardinals.

From the very beginning of the *Exiit qui seminat*, Nicholas III extols the role of the "nourishing confessor Francis;" he emphasizes that the founder received the stigmata of Christ's Passion. He assimilates, as it were, the *Rule*, written by the saint as inspired by God, and the Gospel; it is understandable why John XXII, some fifty

---

[261] Prv 11:14.

[262] Nm 11:16.

[263] John of Wales, *Declaratio super Regulam*, in *Speculum Minorum seu firmamentum trium Ordinum...* (Venice, 1513), f. 103r.

years later, thought he should revoke his predecessor's text. Yet Nicholas III is not unaware of the attacks that the Order of Friars Minor was subjected to and he goes to their aid by proclaiming the sanctity of their vocation. As the general chapter (that of Assisi which, in 1279, completed the *Constitutions* of Narbonne) and the minister general (Bonagrazia de San Giovanni in Persiceto, 1279-1283) asked him to, the pontiff offers to elucidate the last ambiguities of the *Rule*, reminding everyone how perfectly suited he is for doing this, having cherished the Friars Minor from his earliest youth, having conversed with the companions of Francis, and having been cardinal protector of the Order.[264]

The body of the papal constitution closely follows the commentary of Chapters I, VI, IV, II, V, IX, VIII and XI of the *Later Rule*. In fact, the description of the economic conditions of the brothers' life takes up almost all the space.[265] The only institutional point dealt with as such is a literal repeat of the *Quo elongati*: a single custodian will be appointed as a delegate to the general chapter by his peers of the same province. The governance of the Order is incidentally alluded to: the license to preach, which, according to the *Rule*, only the minister general issues, will also be allowed to be dispensed by the provincial ministers gathered in chapter with their definitors; likewise the provincial – indeed his vicar – will be able to examine postulants and admit them to the Order – a

---

[264] Nicholas III, *Exiit qui seminat*, in *Bullarium franciscanum*, 1, 404-06.

[265] Here, as with each reappearance of the theme of poverty that is not within our subject cf. M.D. Lambert, *Franciscan Poverty. The Doctrine of the Absolute Poverty of Christ and the Apostles in the Franciscan Order 1210-1323* (St. Bonaventure, 1998).

simple repetition, this time, of Innocent IV's *Ordinem vestrum*.[266]

Nicholas III, it is believed, is thoroughly familiar with the institutions of the Friars Minor, such as the Chapter of Narbonne had specified them for close to twenty years. He takes note of them and finds nothing at fault; this aspect of the Order was at that time no longer the subject of internal debate, except for that which was provoked by external criticism.

Thus, since Bonaventure's generalate, everything has become dull. The Order is purring along, and the papacy considers the institutional provisions of the *General Constitutions* of 1260 definitive. Then, one generation later, in 1288, the debate is revived with renewed vigor. Some issues that in the past had somehow evaded all discussion are stirred up; others that had never been clearly brought up before are raised. The debate never becomes mainstream, nevertheless more than thirty years apart, it is raised by two authors at odds with the institution: Peter John Olivi and Angelo Clareno.

Peter John Olivi, born in the region of Béziers, enters around the age of twelve, some time around 1260, as a novice in the friary of the Order of Friars Minor of the city. His provincial, a great friend of Hugh of Digne, sends him to the University of Paris. He studies theology there under Bonaventure, but without ever landing the rank of master. He is nevertheless found teaching in various *studia* of Provence, already defending the value that he considers as Franciscan *par excellence* – poverty. In 1279, he collaborates, on this theme, in the doctrinal deliberations preparing the *Exiit qui seminat*, which so strongly emphasizes the parallel between Gospel and *Rule*. In 1282, the masters in theology of the Paris

---

[266] Nicholas III, *Exiit qui seminat*, 414.

studium condemn some of the propositions of his *Commentary on the Sentences,* which he agrees to retract the following year. Deprived of his books and of the very text of the documents that condemn him, he finds both warm supporters and bitter enemies within the Order's hierarchy. From 1287 to 1289, he is appointed lector at the Santa Croce of Florence friary by the new minister general, Matthew of Acquasparta (1287-1289); from here he next moves to Montpellier. From there, his influence expands into lay circles closely related to the Beguines. In 1295, he must again justify his theory of "poor use," which permitted the reconciliation of Franciscan poverty with the enjoyment of goods that were not owned. It is at Narbonne that Peter John Olivi composes his last writings and dies, on March 14, 1298.

His collection of work is considerable – as he leaves a commentary on almost all the books of the Bible – and odd, in many respects. This champion of the most high poverty is at the same time the theorist of "poor use"; this Joachimite – a description with many shades of meaning – who compares the worldly Church, which he nevertheless does not equate with the Roman Church, to the biblical Babylon, is one of the first to affirm papal infallibility. After his death, a part of his doctrine was condemned, without his being named, at the Council of Vienna in 1311-1312, and his *Commentary on the Apocalypse* was later censured by John XXII, in 1326.

According to his editor, David Flood, the *Rule Commentary* was composed in the second half of 1288.[267] Eleven manuscripts (five from the fourteenth century, four from the fifteenth, two from the beginning of the sixteenth century) and one 1513 edition each contain

---

[267] D. Flood, *Peter Olivi's Rule Commentary*; Id., "Pierre Jean Olivi et la Règle franciscaine," in *Franciscains d'Oc: les "Spirituels" (1280-1325)*, Cahiers de Fanjeaux, 10 (Toulouse, 1975), 139-54.

the text, which was therefore not intended for a narrow readership. In his prologue,[268] Peter John Olivi presents this commentary as the practical complement of his theoretical treatise on *Questions on Evangelical Perfection*. He notes that the text of the *Rule* is truly the one that Francis produced, that, from the first chapter, "he is put forward by name as the general leader of the Order and as its original teacher," and that, everywhere else, he intervenes in the first person. He stresses the successive papal approvals.

In the commentary of Chapter I,[269] the author observes that it is no surprise that this "evangelical *Rule*," following from the teaching of Christ, encourages obedience to the Vicar of Christ and the Roman Church. Going back to the Pauline images of the head and the members, he finds that one of the Order's foundations is the obedience due to the minister general, adding that the subsidiary superiors in no way play a part in "a diminishment of the power [*potestatis*] of the general, or as a distancing factor between subordinates and him, but act only as a support for him." Just as the pope is the customary and direct leader of all Christians, so is the general for the Order of Minors. Commenting on the expression, "*Regula et vita fratrum minorum*," Olivi emphasizes the direct evangelical inspiration of the written work in question; observance of the *Rule* and of the Gospel are one and the same. Our author, who is particularly sensitive to the usage of the terms *vita* or *vivere* in the Franciscan text, adds that the real superior of the friars is Christ and that the life of the Minors defined by the *Rule*, with its three vows, is nothing other than

---

[268] Peter John Olivi, *Expositio super Regulam fratrum minorum*, ed. D. Flood, *Peter Olivi's Rule Commentary*, 114-15.
[269] Id., *ibid.*, 116-22.

the fulfillment of the evangelical life. All the brothers owe obedience to Francis, who owes obedience to the pope, which means that all owe obedience to the pope, and, through him, to Christ. But the nominal reference to Francis is not immaterial; a community that followed the same way of life but is not answerable to his legitimate successor would be a different one from the Order of Friars Minor, for Francis received the seal of the stigmata and he is, like the angel of the sixth seal, "the one who renews the life of Christ" – a theme dear to Peter John Olivi, to which he will return in his conclusion.[270]

As is done throughout his treatise, the commentary that our author gives of Chapter VIII of the *Rule*[271] is striking in its concern for detail – doubly so, in fact: detail of the scholastic form, and detail of the answers provided to all the questions that may arise in the daily life of the Order. But it is characteristic of this demanding scholastic thought that it raises, in a systematic way, unforeseen and innovative questions which may turn out to be fraught with consequences.

First, Peter John Olivi notes that it is every brother who is always bound to have a minister general and, consequently, that in case the ministers and custodians should be reluctant to hold an election, everyone must push for it. The obedience owed to the general is evoked. Next, the delegation of a custodian to represent those of his province at the general chapter is again mentioned. According to the custom of the Order and a papal decision (*Ad statum* of May 13, 1288, which allows the editor to date the *Commentary* of the Languedoc friar with precision), the custodian delegate has only a single vote. This is logical, judges our author, since, otherwise, a single custodian could have more weight than seven or

---

[270] Id., *ibid.*, 194-96.
[271] Id., *ibid.*, 178-83.

eight ministers. This limit on the number of custodians is therefore in no way contrary to the spirit of the *Rule*. In doing this, Olivi recognizes that the original text could not consider all the problems presented afterwards by the vast number of friars and that it is therefore licit to complete it by statutes.

We must remember here that the principle of the custodians' representation, defined by Gregory IX in *Quo elongati* of 1230, reaffirmed by Innocent IV and Nicholas III in *Ordinem vestrum* of 1245 and *Exiit qui seminat* of 1279, respectively, and which no longer seemed to pose a problem at this latter date, had nevertheless been contested by the General Chapter of Montpellier in 1287. The assembly had on the contrary proposed the following alternative: that all custodians be again allowed into the general chapter, or that each "custodian of custodians" have a mandate equal to the number of individuals he represents. In 1288, through *Ad statum*, Nicholas IV (1288-1292), the first Friar Minor to become pope, ruled out both possibilities.[272] It is precisely this position that Peter John Olivi confirms in his *Commentary*.

The fact, continues our author, that the power to dismiss the general is entrusted by the *Rule* to the general chapter is proof that the minister is subject to the assembly. Obedience is thus very much owed to the minister, but under the condition that he doesn't go "against the *Rule* and against the soul," nor against the statutes enacted by the chapter. This is a point, emphasizes Olivi, in keeping with what the *General Constitutions* of the Order (those of Narbonne, of course) declare when they indicate, from the very beginning, that the Order's principal governmental authority resides in the general chapter. The Four Masters may also be cited in support of this. However, the expression "against the *Rule* and

---

[272] Marinus a Neukirchen, *De capitulo generali* ..., 109-10.

against the soul" calls to mind another source, which is not made explicit by the author: the *Earlier Rule*, which anticipated the case of a minister's commanding "one of the brothers to do something against our life or his soul."[273] The changing of statutes may thus not "be left to the will of the general [*arbitrio generalis*]" without taking into account the opinion of the chapter. But if a decision of the general made "against the *Rule* or against the soul" can have no binding force, a statute of the chapter which would be tainted with the same weaknesses no longer constrains the general or the Order. This, we see, is to make the *Rule* – in reality, the interpretation of it that each one can make in all conscience – fit to oppose superiors as well as group authority.

For the election and the deposing of the general, the majority of the votes plus one is required. On the possible causes for the deposing of the superior, Peter John Olivi mentions two contradictory opinions: for one group, the situation comes up only if he has demonstrated his inadequacy (with regard to the common good, our author later emphasizes); for the other group, he may also be deposed if he requests it, or if he may be more useful in another office, provided that he is replaced by someone equally or more capable than he. Olivi notes the fluctuations in names in the *Rule* between custodian, minister general, and provincial. There are some, he adds, who consider that there is no reason to obey guardians, since they are not even named in the *Rule*. But this is incorrect: a community of friars cannot be without a local superior, and all superiors given by the minister – general or provincial – must be obeyed, according to the arrangement of the general chapter; the term "minister" is generic in the Franciscan texts and applies therefore as well to guardians, whose name is

---

[273] ER 5:2.

nothing other than the common translation of the Latin
custos; finally, the tradition of the Order, confirmed by
popes, has established it as such. Here, our author is four
years ahead of the 1292 Paris Chapter, which will clearly
acknowledge guardians as having the title of superior.

With particular insistence – four references to the
New Testament and two to the Old – Peter John Olivi
emphasizes that every prelate of the Order has received
an evangelical name – bearer of humility – with the
responsibility of service and not that of peaceful sinecure.
But he also brings to the fore, with a sharp critical look,
the aporias of the *Rule*: nothing says whether the elected
general must consent to his election, whether it must
be confirmed by the pope or whether the election and
the consent of the interested party suffice; nothing
specifies the modes of procedure and it is not known
whether it must be done by ballot, compromise or divine
inspiration (we recognize here the categories of Canon
24 of the Fourth Lateran Council). From this, it must
therefore be concluded that it is left to the discretion of
the general chapter "in conformity with common law."
In the end, it must be understood that the electorate is in
full possession of the weight of the general chapter only
for the election or the deposing of the general and that,
for the rest, they cannot do without the presence of the
minister, or his approval and his authority in the event
of absence.

Despite these technical flaws, Olivi concludes that
the *Rule* instituted "a very useful mode of government:"

> This system of government is very effectual,
> according to the pagan philosopher Aristotle as
> well, since it is monarchical and yet everyone
> participates together in some way. Just as the unity
> of the head truly guards against scission, it is also
> easier to find a single very wise person who excels

at governing than a great number; likewise, one person sees things better, in a more thoughtful and mature manner, if he is supported by the counsel of many others than if he is alone.

What is more, that which was conceived of through the advice, and has received the consent, of all or of the majority is more readily respected; here we recognize an echo of John of Wales's argumentation. The multitude, supervised by the head and by others, is more fearful of differences, while the head, supervised by others, is kept from doing wrong and behaves more prudently. Furthermore, the fact that the friars converge on the chapter from many regions allows them, by emulation, to progress in virtue and then to spread widely the statutes and customs of the Order. However, it is true that, if they gather and share their bad examples, innumerable evils and the stench of vice may follow. There where John of Wales saw only a happy arrangement, our author cannot help from also considering ill-fated consequences.

It is difficult to measure exactly the effect of Peter John Olivi's remarks on the constitutional aspects of the Order of Friars Minor. It is difficult to judge it impartially, disregarding the consequences that the inquisitions into his writings had on those that followed. This is exactly where all the difficulty continues to lie in evaluating the work of the Languedoc friar on its own. Such indeed is the paradox: Olivi's conclusions are in perfect conformity with all that had been established by the best-known tradition of the Order, but the issues that his investigative and speculative mind confronts before arriving at these classic conclusions raise many questions that will have to be considered after he is gone! Let us look closely at these two aspects.

To compare the Franciscan *Rule* with the Gospel will certainly displease John XXII, but, at the time that our author writes his *Commentary*, it is an analogy perfectly in keeping with *Exiit qui seminat* of Nicholas III, with whose content Olivi was moreover not unfamiliar. To present Francis in an apocalyptic light is a daring move that Thomas of Celano, in the *Treatise on the Miracles*, and Bonaventure, in the *Major Legend*, had allowed themselves, before our perennial suspect. The latter, moreover, from a strictly disciplinary standpoint, doesn't stop insisting on the obedience owed by the brothers to the Roman Church, to the pope, to the minister general – holder of the *potestas* – and to the guardians. Like the Four Masters and the *Constitutions* of 1260, he recognizes the higher *auctoritas* of the general chapter, in a very Bonaventurian synthesis which seems to be approved unanimously just after the Chapter of Narbonne. On questions of procedure, both the majority ballot and the delegation of a custodian representing his peers are recognized as perfectly valid, the former in agreement with canon law, the latter with the positions of four pontiffs – Gregory IX, Innocent IV, Nicholas III, and Nicholas IV – and without the least accommodation for the protest expressed at the Montpellier Chapter in 1287. It is impossible to be more respectful of the principle and the decisions of authority.

However, Peter John Olivi – in one respect because of his uncompromising evangelism, and in another respect through his desire to justify everything logically, thus to explore all the possibilities before making a decision – sows permanent doubt. In the first place and outside the Order, the hierarchical position of the pope – caught between Christ, whose vicar he is, and a saint who, because he had received the seal of the stigmata directly from God, is compared with the angel of the sixth seal – is anything but comfortable. In the second place and within the Order, the selection of the general is entrusted to the attention of all the brothers and no longer to the sole jurisdiction of the chapter; the will of the minister is subject to the requirement of faithfulness to the *Rule* and to the good of the soul, of which each one may consider himself to be the interpreter – thus to the judgment of each one, that is to say of all, and no longer to the control of the one chapter that has the right to depose him. Now since, at the same time, it is emphasized that nothing in the *Rule* defines the electoral procedures and that interpretations other than the papal one may arise concerning the presence of the custodians in chapter, it is the entire constitutional structure of the Order that is shaken. Olivi's classic conclusions – sincere beyond a doubt, but arrived at through a process of free thinking that may at any moment be termed unorthodox – seem in fact to be the last coat of plaster thrown over unintended cracks.

And then, there is the first explicit reference, in this literature, to the *Politics* of Aristotle. In itself, the allusion is vague; it probably corresponds to the means proposed by the Stagirite to ensure the preservation of the monarchical system of government, in Book V of his work.[274] But it does not appear alone. The passage of the *Commentary* which immediately follows, we remember, is thus argued:

> It is also easier to find a single very wise person who excels at governing than a great number.

In Book III of *Politics*, Aristotle writes:

> It is possible for a single individual or a small number to grow in virtue; on the other hand it is

---

[274] Aristotle, *Politics*, V:11.

difficult for a more considerable number of men to attain perfection.[275]

Let's admit it: there is nothing revolutionary in the content of the two borrowings, explicit or implicit, that Peter John Olivi makes from Greek philosophy. But their appearance is an event in itself. It could hardly have happened earlier; *Politics* was only translated into Latin in 1260. Until then, concerning the aspects that interest us, the entire reference system which underlay the reflection on the institution of the Order of Friars Minor had remained internal to the religious culture: the superior authority of the Scriptures, the re-employment of Augustine or Jerome, Gregory the Great, Bernard of Clairvaux or Hugh of St. Victor, the explicit canonical scope of the Fourth Lateran Council, the implicit influence of the normative elaborations of the Cistercians and the Preachers, the Franciscan *Rules*, and the specific string of *Rule Commentaries* and the papal letters applying to them.

For the first time, a writer external to this closed system – a "pagan philosopher," emphasizes Peter John Olivi, who by the way is not very fond of either Aristotle or Averroes and denounces their use in the teaching of theology – is called upon for help. He is not used – let us carefully note – as an authority in the strict sense, enabling us to make decisions, or to legitimately base our opinions on him, but as a simple explanatory reference. The constitutional principles of the Order are good because they are determined by the *Rule* of the angel of the sixth seal; furthermore, it happens that they mention what Aristotle says of a monarchy tempered by the participation of the greatest number. It is a minor

---

[275] Id., *ibid.*, III:7.

point, certainly, but one which interrupts the peaceful operation of a working system.

This is how Peter John Olivi – author of undeniable fidelity to the Church, who remains disconcerted at the critical disapproval he raises throughout his life – is able to undermine completely the structures that he defends. He is suspected of having begun the era of suspicion.

Our last author, Angelo Clareno, renders to the man from Languedoc the formidable service of making him into his predecessor. Peter of Fossombrone enters the Order of Friars Minor around 1270, where he takes the name of Angelo Clareno. He first becomes famous through his stance in favor of radical poverty. Put in prison, he is set free in 1290. He leaves for Cilicia, returns to Italy in 1294 and, in the company of Peter of Macerata – that is, Brother Liberato – he then receives the oral authorization from Pope Celestin V (1294) to create the autonomous congregation of the "Hermits of Pope Celestin," who claim to adhere to the teachings of Francis but apart from the Order of Minors. Olivi definitely would not have liked this at all. For Angelo Clareno, the abdication of the old hermit-become-pontiff and the election of Boniface VIII (1294-1303) mark the rebirth of trouble. He takes refuge in Greece for ten years, where he translates numerous Eastern monastic writings from Greek to Latin. Returning to Italy in 1307, he goes next to Avignon in 1311, in the court of Cardinal Jacques Colonna, and attempts to obtain written recognition of the Poor Hermits. The letter *Exivi de Paradiso*, published by Clement V (1305-1314) in 1312, seems to him, in the line of *Exiit qui seminat*, to come closest to the founder's intention. Then comes the election of John XXII (1316-1334), who, through *Sancta romana* of December 30, 1317, condemns the rebellious Spirituals under the name "Fraticelli (little friars)." Angelo Clareno is thrown permanently in with the dissidents. He takes refuge in the Benedictine Monastery of Subiaco from 1318 to 1334, from where he influences the fraticelli communities of Italy, and then flees to Basilicata where he dies, on June 15, 1337. He leaves an extensive correspondence and a *History of the Seven Tribulations,* written around 1326, in which he relates his version of the trials undergone by the Order begun by Francis.

The *Commentary on the Rule of Friars Minor,* dedicated to an unknown Brother Thomas, was written by Angelo Clareno around 1321-1322. At that time the dissident Spirituals had already been condemned for four or five years. The author himself must have been taking refuge in Subiaco. Five manuscripts of it are known: two from the fourteenth century, two from the fifteenth, and one from the sixteenth, of which four are found in Rome and one in Munich. The work is voluminous, multiform, and strewn with references to both Eastern and Western Fathers, developing lengthy comparisons with other monastic institutions as well as between the two preserved Franciscan *Rules*; it includes episodes from the life of Francis taken from the tradition of Brother Leo's writings, along the way supplying details that were previously unpublished – and to some extent unfounded – like the formal announcement by Innocent III of his recognition of the Franciscan *Rule* at the Fourth Lateran Council.

The commentary of Chapter VIII[276] focuses first on the role of the minister general. He must be a good shepherd, conforming "in all things to Christ, the good shepherd." He must be "the last of all and the servant of all." There was a time when this short refrain, stressed in a long citation from the *Second Life* describing the ideal

---

[276] Angelo Clareno, *Expositio super Regulam fratrum minorum,* ed. G. Boccali, introd. F. Accrocca, Ital. trans. M. Bigaroni, Pubblicazioni della Biblioteca francescana, Chiesa nuova, 7 (Assisi, 1994), 606-28.

minister general,[277] had not been understood.[278] The definition of the minister by Angelo Clareno, similar to that of Hugh of Digne, is essentially a moral, evangelical – in fact Franciscan – one, nevertheless imbued with the Eastern ascetical and monastic tradition.

The author next compares the minister general to the Sovereign Pontiff: to the first is owed the obedience of all the friars, to the second, of all the faithful. The comparison doesn't end there. The election of the minister by the chapter is compared to the election of the pontiff by the cardinals. Yet, adds the Spiritual, if the cardinals are prevented from doing so, it is up to the bishops, the other Christian princes and the entire clergy to provide themselves with a shepherd. Likewise, if the ministers and custodians are prevented from electing the minister, the friars must put their energy into getting a general. Here we recognize the viewpoint of Peter John Olivi. The modes of election are not specified.

The designation of only one custodian per province, according to the dictates of *Quo elongati*, seems to Angelo Clareno to be contrary to literal respect for the *Rule*. He thus distances himself here from his spiritual father to agree with the stance of the 1287 Montpellier General Chapter. Quite a few custodians, he argues, are the equivalent of ministers and a chapter which would gather them all would not exceed four hundred brothers. In 1334 Benedict XII (1334-1342) will state his verdict: unchangeable respect for *Quo elongati*. Beyond the specific situation, what Angelo Clareno puts into question is the very possibility of modifying the founding text in any way, thus moving away from the more realistic considerations of Peter John Olivi. The Italian Spiritual

---

[277] 2C 185-186.

[278] Cf. again Angelo Clareno, *Expositio super Regulam*, 644-50, with a long citation from ER.

also mentions that the chapter has the power to legislate, that its decisions bind all the brothers – especially the superiors – and that, while it is the minister general who convokes the chapter, it is the chapter that surfaces the name of and potentially deposes the minister. Finally, it is in the *Earlier Rule* that our author will find the image that seems to him the most eloquent for defining "the minister and servant" – that of the mutual washing of feet.[279]

All things considered, the traditional reminder of the predominance of the legislative over the executive does not preclude, in the interpretation that Angelo Clareno makes of the *Rule*, an increase in the moral value of the ministerial function. By questioning the delegation of power made to a custodian by others from the same province, the author challenges what appeared in 1230 to be an advance in representativeness. Yet perhaps, without doing any technical analysis of it, he has the intuition, following the friars of the Montpellier Chapter, that, since 1242, the appointment of the custodians had been the sensitive spot in the institutional structure of the Order of Friars Minor. The dissident Spiritual, in doing this, challenges especially the Apostolic See on one of the rare constitutional points where the papacy and the Order had experienced a divergence since 1287. The comparison between papal election and election of the minister, which could still seem – and probably was – innocuous with Peter John Olivi, here seems full of hidden meanings: to speak of a right of the entire clergy and the princes to take control, in some ways, of a pope's accession can no longer be a totally innocent remark after the discussions on the validity of the resignation of Celestine V and the consequent election of Boniface VIII in 1294.

---

[279] ER 6:3-4.

With the dissident Spiritual, who is preoccupied with a genuine return to Franciscan origins with an instinctive preference for the older of the two preserved *Rules* and for the biographical accounts of Brother Leo, there is definitely a nostalgia for "direct democracy" linked to a charismatic leader: hadn't it been this way until the early 1220's? With that – clearly going backwards in comparison to Peter John Olivi, who is at the same time the heir of the earlier normative elaboration that he drives to the wall and, by that very act, the one who sparks the later debates that disregard him –, Angelo Clareno demonstrates a relative negligence towards the strictly institutional aspects, which is not the least of his similarities to the beginnings of the Order. We must again read through the beginnings of the movement that is called, with never enough qualifications, "spiritual" in this perspective, by returning to the *solemnes fratres* in revolt against the Minister General Crescentius of Jesi (1244-1247) and their denial of all authority in the Order. A return to the sources, which is also a reversal of direction with respect to a century of patient institutional construction based on an original *aporia* – this is truly the beauty, the limitation and the drama of the history of the Spirituals.

Chapter Three

The End of the Journey

More than conclusions, these are the few observations that come to mind at the end of this study.

A Short Note on Methodology

Throughout this study, we have desired to respect the particular nature of each source which seemed helpful to our reflection and to avoid a synthetic analysis which would have engendered the replacement of a process of internal interpretation of the texts with the institutional itinerary that led to the Order of Friars Minor in general, then by the history of the Order of Friars Minor from 1206 to 1260. Each person thus has at his disposal the material that would allow him to make his own possible interpretation.

This choice rests on the conviction that, at least at the beginning of the study, the very fruitful method defined by Arsenio Frugoni in the case of Arnold of Brescia[1] is worthwhile not only for biographical sources, but for all types of documents. In the attempt to understand

---

[1] A. Frugoni, *Arnaldo da Brescia nelle fonti del sec. XII*, Studi storici, 8-9 (Rome, 1954); P. Toubert, "Histoire et réforme ecclésiastique en Italie au XIe et au XIIe siècles. À propos de deux études récentes," *Revue des études italiennes*, n.s. 8 (1961): 64-71.

an historical personage, a synthetic analysis results in the smoothing out of the individual, a filing down of his or her inconsistencies. Should such an approach be used to understand the evolution of an institution, it would result in skirting to a great degree around the richness of an ideological debate. Now, as we leave these sources, evidence emerges that there was an ideological debate in the Order of Friars Minor on the central issue of government from 1220 to 1260, definitely in the years afterwards, and probably beforehand as well. And while the outcome of this maturation is most certainly not immaterial, the terms of the discussion are just as interesting, as a persistent exploration of all possibilities.

To take just one example, the balance of power finally achieved in 1260 between minister and chapter is a remarkable achievement; yet, the usage of the terms *auctoritas* and *potestas*, each in their appropriate contexts, must have been emphasized as well.

FRANCIS, THE INSTITUTION, THE GOVERNMENT

In spite of these excellent principles, we have expressed what were often unkind opinions regarding our "principal" (in the etymological sense) personage. Was it necessary to stoop to speaking of Francis as a dissatisfied megalomaniac, an autocrat imposing his dictates through his "demagogic" skill, a person incapable of dialoguing with his brothers and of accepting other points of view besides his own, alternately using threats and emotional blackmail...?

It has been understood, we hope, that these obviously excessive remarks in no way dampen a genuine empathy for Francis and that it is not a question of lecturing a man who has been dead for almost eight hundred years, and canonized by the Church on top of it. This type of provocation is only helpful when the weight of accepted images becomes a real hindrance to reflection, or even to historical research. Now, the conventional view on Francis's humility, consistently held by the sources – in particular the autobiographical and hagiographical ones – is often intended to conceal or smooth over decisive historical developments. The real problem arises only from the fact that this representation, which calcifies the mind, is taken up over and over again by the great majority of modern authors, including those who should practice and teach critical reading. So many biographers, with touching tremors in the writing, have extolled the humility and simplicity of the Poverello, without ever suspecting they could have contained some moralizing. It is difficult to understand logically why such a reproach is valid only in the case of negative moral judgments.

To put forward – in a joking manner, of course – a moral judgment that contradicts the accepted pious image only serves to draw attention to the inconsistencies of the historical personage in question. Of these, there is an overabundance.

For example, one could present Francis alternately as an ingenious idealist manipulated by the Church – God knows that this image is not lacking! – or as a realist very clear about his objectives, who knows how to make use of the support of the Roman See when he needs to. Brother Leo's presentation is certainly favored by most, but one should not disregard the presentation made in the *Life of Gregory IX* without a closer look. Is it the naked truth in one place, and shameless propaganda in the other? Based on what criteria, on which critical method?

Is Francis the enemy of institutionalization, unfurling the little flag of the fraternity against the big banner of the Order? This is certainly no wild invention of the imagination. It is the apparently scientifically indisputable lesson of the lexicology and the obvious message of the *Testament*. But a Francis on the road to Rome with his ridiculous group, breaking through barriers to reach the Sovereign Pontiff, ready to extend his influence to France, ordering the conquest of Germany, asking for a protector with the rank of cardinal, spending the greater part of his religious life concocting a normative text, agreeing on two occasions that he personally should be the linchpin which would connect the submission and the subordination of thousands of brothers to the pope: is this a purely theoretical view, a malicious invention, or are they facts clearly established from independent and corroborating sources, according to the method defined by John Mabillon? "Did St. Francis exist?" wondered Edward of Alençon.[2] One cannot help asking, on the same note, "did the Order of Friars Minor exist?" Yet the great subtlety of Francis is to make us believe, counter to what Louis XIV said of the State, that "He is not the Order."

Indeed, the institutional negligence of the founder may be demonstrated without the slightest difficulty, and the *aporias* in the *Later Rule* have not failed to make an impression. Isn't this flagrant proof of the lack of interest in any kind of system a sign of preference for function over form, for the spiritual over the administrative? Yes, the system, the administration – who would ever claim to like them? Poor Martha – that meal served to Christ cost her more than she would have imagined in the working out of her small household accounts! Yet Elias, who goes so far as to neglect convoking the chapter: doesn't he teach us that negligence can be a method of government, and not exactly one of those methods that offers the most guarantees to those who are governed? From what we

---

[2] Édouard d'Alençon, "Saint François a-t-il existé?," *Études franciscaines*, 15 (1906): 481-95.

can see of the way the chapters were run in the founder's day, would those making the friars' appointments to such-and-such an office have put up with arithmetically defined procedures for deliberation and designation? Francis claims to have a mandate from God. This time, paraphrasing Joseph Vissarionovitch Djougachvili, it is tempting to ask, "God, how many votes?" To confuse institutional with charismatic power, like confusing family with institution, is never innocently done.

The resignation of Francis: could we dream of a more impressive backwards achievement? Just how far will the stripping of self go? Other founders than the Umbrian penitent have relinquished their office as superior of the institute established by their efforts. The man from Assisi thus does not make an original gesture – he falls within a typology.[3] Again, we need to shake off the hypnosis of the "new Franciscan movement" and take the trouble to review the theory of these early retirements. Of course, the resigning founder very specifically renounces only a certain right to oversee the institute that rose from his works. Regarding this sort of thing, it would even seem that religious founders possessed less virtue and reserve than political founders, such as Sylla, Charles Quint, Charles De Gaulle, etc.

The distinction that was established at Fontevrault, from October 28, 1115 to February 25, 1116, between Robert of Arbrissel, the founder of the double abbey near Saumur, and Petronilla of Chemillé, the abbess designated to take his place at the head of the men and women of the religious institute, seems to have had a sound basis: Petronilla had the effective power, Robert the spiritual

---

[3] J. Dalarun, "La mort des saints fondateurs, de Martin à François," in *Les fonctions des saints dans le monde occidental (IIIe-XIIIe siècle). Actes du colloque organisé par l'École française de Rome avec le concours de l'Université de Rome "La Sapienza", Rome, 27-29 octobre 1988*, Collection de l'École française de Rome, 149 (Rome, 1991), 193-215.

authority – an authority which gained in prestige what it may have lost in efficiency.[4] Perhaps Robert's good luck was in not living too long after his retirement, but we do not see Francis agreeing to a similar departure. The very hesitation over the exact title of his substitutes – vicars or minister generals[5] – throughout not only historiography, but also the early Franciscan sources, which are for this reason unable to arrive at any coherent count of the number of generals,[6] speaks sufficient volumes on the issue. Therefore, we have not attempted to resolve it, for the fact that there is a dilemma is, in this dilemma, the most enlightening element, in that this impossible distinction reflects the indecisiveness of Francis. In so many ways, the founder could not make up his mind.

No matter what moral attribute is linked to it, no matter what anthropological figure expresses it, we cannot deny that there was an exercise of power on Francis's part before 1220. We can wonder about the exact meaning of his resignation – was it humility, fatigue, a feeling of defeat – against what? –, a desire to check a development that was getting away from him by a striking, almost desperate, gesture? But what must be noted above all, as a fact consistently based on the sources, is that this exercise of power did not cease after 1220 and, consequently, we can only wonder if there were temptations toward the abuse of power on the part of the resigning founder after this date – not with respect to any type of moralism, but with respect to a decision

---

[4] Id., "Pouvoir et autorité dans l'Ordre double de Fontevraud," in *Les religieuses dans le cloître et dans le monde*, 335-51.

[5] C. Schmitt, "I vicari dell'Ordine francescano da Pietro Cattani a frate Elia," in *Francesco d'Assisi e francescanesimo dal 1216 al 1226. Atti del IV convegno internazionale, Assisi, 15-17 ottobre 1976* (Assisi, 1977), 235-63.

[6] R. Brooke, *Early Franciscan Government* ...., 110-11.

that could never be claimed to have been directly forced by anyone.

After so many edifying paraphrases of the *Testament*, Grado Merlo had the audacity to shatter the unanimous opinion and instruct us to see "the harshness of Francis"[7] there, as well. "What does *Testament* mean?" wonders Giovanni Miccoli in the commendable interpretation of it that he proposes.[8] It is tempting to add, "what, then, does 'to dictate his last wishes' mean?" What, at this point, would be of such importance to write about that hadn't been possible to accomplish? What concept of self and of others does that convey? What concept of self and of one's death, of self and of the present time, of self and of the time that, along with others, follows us?

Through all the studies of Francis's life, there have continued to be two possible interpretations; of these, the negative one, by design, was always pushed to the fore in an attempt simply to have it acknowledged as a possibility. The moment when Paul Sabatier, the prodigious pioneer who was able to revive the lifeless Franciscan documents, resolved the dilemma by distributing the roles among the saint's companions was a rewarding one, but that is in the past. It was helpful, but it is no longer convincing to think that Elias, Hugolino or Thomas of Celano were pulling a founder completely bewildered by the situation in one direction while Leo and the companions were pulling him in the other. If we agree to choose our sources based only on the level of information they provide and not by the fact that they promote some ideological prejudice or other, if we choose to listen to all sources that are equal in value for

---

[7] G.G. Merlo, *Tra eremo e città. Studi su Francesco d'Assisi e sul francescanesimo*, Saggi, 2 (Assisi, 1991), 36-40.

[8] G. Miccoli, *Il Testamento di san Francesco*.

what they say and not for what we expect to hear, we must recognize that, in the majority of contradictory interpretations proposed above, taking into account the sources' typology, the author's preferences, and the context in which they were written, each of the two ways of understanding has – at the very least – the right to be considered. We must also recognize that, by the same token, chances are that these contradictions existed to a great degree in Francis personally.

But aren't we speaking too much of Francis specifically and therefore succumbing to the extremely personalized version of the founding of the Order of Friars Minor that was given, almost unanimously, by the medieval sources? For the *tour de force* is that the man from Assisi seems to accept the institution only regretfully, yet he seems at the same time to be its indisputable instructor. David Flood pointed out insistently and with conviction that a history of the fraternity could not be compiled based on the lone figure of the founder, but that it was necessary to rediscover the collective dimension of this original group experience and to understand it as being as much a product of the companions as of Francis.[9] Very good. Certainly it is necessary, more than once, in one or another hagiographic representation, to mentally replace "the blessed father" with the group of companions, as is frequently done, by the way, in the *Anonymous of Perugia*. But the confusion comes from the fact that even the moments presented as occurring in a group in the hagiographical sources or the chronicles do not in reality focus on the group, which makes us think that the saint's hagiographers were not the only ones, nor the

---

[9] For example D. Flood, *Francis of Assisi and the Franciscan Movement* (Quezon City, Philippines, 1989), 149 ss.

first, to give him all the credit. Thus what the sources have to say about the chapters held during Francis's lifetime seem hardly to show any real consultation or fraternal dialogue. Regarding the *Testament*, it is written in not only an autobiographical style, but in a strongly "egotistical" one as well. The pronoun *ego* recurs twenty-one times. And how can we go the way judiciously pointed out by David Flood if each time a protagonist other than Francis is bold enough to intervene in the Order's development, we take him for a manipulator or a traitor?

Were the vicars traitors who, taking advantage of the journey to the East in 1220, wished to impose the monastic fast and allowed privileges to pile up? Were the brothers traitors who, in 1222, wished to return to the wisdom of the traditional *Rules*? Were the brothers renegades who went to the pope in 1230, asking to be freed from the oppressive tutelage that came from living in the great shadow of the deceased? But – we will say – those are not the brothers we must look to, to try to find echoes of the original experience, but to the companions, in the oldest layers of the *Earlier Rule*. Must we abandon an Order's history as seen through the founder's image, the fruit of an unrestrained personality cult, only to succumb to a similar "idol of the beginnings," to give ourselves over to the same type of "embryonic obsession"?[10] Does all the experience gained after 1220 then mean nothing? Christ was not this harsh to the workers who arrived in the last hour.

---

[10] M. Bloch, *Apologie pour l'histoire ou métier d'historien* (Paris, 1949), 5-9.

A Short Historiographical Note

The Franciscan sources, shaped by the contradictions of Francis of Assisi, have themselves provided a great deal of information for historiography. Let's be quite clear about this: we cannot advocate reading the sources for what they have to say and at the same time reproach historians for repeating them. However, a critical mind – which most certainly would not encourage a rejection of the sources, but which also could not condone an acceptance of only their superficial meaning – is, as a rule, also required. Thus, it is particularly disturbing to see the near unanimity with which the words of the writings and the legends on the humility of Francis are taken up literally by the majority of authors. It is also very troubling to see how the insistence on the choice of minority would allow the acceptance and – why does the word still frighten us? – the deliberate choice, by the man from Assisi, of the institutionalization of the fraternity into an Order to be easily put into the background. Just as much could be said of all the pages written on the "drama of Francis," which copy what the sources are only too happy to tell us, or on the sublimation of this same drama and the internal lacerations of the Order by the impression of the stigmata; these are nothing other than the almost word-for-word repetitions of what Thomas of Celano tells us from the *First Life* onwards.

It is striking, we repeat, to see that the Franciscan dossier, which has given rise to a labor of noteworthy criticism like few others, was nevertheless able to make the image of Francis that it wished to present widely accepted at face value, that it was able – as if possessing the skill of a ventriloquist – to make the most diverse scholars say what it wanted them to say. No particular modern author is meant here. Or rather, yes – the writer of these lines thinks that, in his brief Franciscan-related existence, he has made most of the remarks that have just been called to mind....

Now, because Francis seems to say that the institution is unimportant, the history of the institution begun by Francis has been overwhelmingly neglected. As always, the exceptions – and they are excellent ones, moreover – prove the rule: Gratien de Paris, Rosalind Brooke, John Moorman, Théophile Desbonnets, David Flood, Giulia Barone, and a few others. But these are so few in number in comparison to the ocean of studies that make every effort to resolve the "Franciscan question"! The pious vow, so often made and always unfulfilled, according to which must be rewritten Gratien de Paris's *Histoire de la fondation et de l'évolution de l'Ordre des frères mineurs au XIIIe siècle (History of the foundation and evolution of the Order of Friars Minor in the Thirteenth Century)* is significant – just as it is significant that the need has been felt to reprint the work fifty-four years later with helpful updating, since we see no successor to him coming along.

The recent discovery by Cesar Cenci of *Constitutions* written prior to those of Narbonne should have been the subject of great discussion. Hadn't it often been lamented – in passing, it is true – that there was almost no trace of any legislation prior to Bonaventure? This is not to deprecate the remarkable find of that great scholar, Cesar Cenci – quite the opposite – but to note that until now it has not enjoyed the mention it deserves.[11] Let us imagine for a moment the ripple of interest that would have passed through the circle of specialists if the original manuscript of the collection of the brothers' memories accompanying the *Letter of Greccio* had been found!

---

[11] Also, I must especially thank Luigi Pellegrini for bringing this publication to my attention.

The Casanatense double leaf makes us advance twenty-one years – in reverse, of course – in the knowledge of the legislation of the Order of Friars Minor. Truly an enormous leap.

The contribution of the double leaf cannot be measured only by number of years. It contributes, like all of this institutional history for which it is henceforth an essential reference, to a powerful clarification of the internal debates of the Order of Friars Minor. These debates, which we will go back over, were lively, precise, subtle and fundamental at the same time. They reveal positions and divisions that the hagiographic sources, overwhelmingly preferred in the studies of Francis, only barely allow to be caught sight of. Under the influence, for the most part, of the Spiritual writers of the early fourteenth century, there has been an obsession, not without the risk of anachronism, with the divisions – deduced by using the regressive method – between community and zealots. We have said all that was possible to say of the famous debate on the interpretation of poverty. It would not be a question of denying, by sheer reaction, the importance of these distinctions. But is it difficult to believe that the way of governing five to twenty thousand individuals spread throughout all the known world[12] did not also excite some interest, give rise to a variety of viewpoints, and bring about divisions and reassemblings, for which an attempt must be made to understand how they are linked – by being completely or partially superimposed, or on the contrary, without corresponding in the least – with the other debates that were barely brought up and which have held more of our attention.

---

[12] L. Pellegrini, *I quadri e i tempi...*

THE ORDER, THE NORM, THE DEBATE

The institutional development that began to ferment in 1230 and that meets with clear success in 1260, but yet doesn't stop there, reveals itself in two connected yet distinct ways. On one hand, the institution, formless at the start, is more precisely defined and organized by efficient normative texts. On the other hand, on the fringe of this gradual construction of the norm, writers present their viewpoints and advance their opinions, most often under the form of commentaries on the Franciscan *Rule* in a climate that must truly be described as one of relative "freedom of expression." We describe it in this way because the most recent of the authors taken into consideration, Angelo Clareno, composed his *Commentary* even though his positions had been clearly condemned as deviant by the Sovereign Pontiff and he did so while still openly and publicly living in a famous Benedictine monastery located at a two days' walk from the See – deserted, it's true – of the Roman Church. Let us therefore begin with the outcome of the whole normative evolution, before returning to the subtleties of the opposing arguments.

On the first point, that part of the overall statutory evolution of the Friars Minor which is connected with the government of the Order – the *Rules* preserved in the *Constitutions* of Narbonne – could be aphoristically summarized in this way: the governance becomes "democratic" when the selection of candidates ceases to be "popular." But that implies that we ask ourselves about the terms "democratic" and "popular."

In occasionally using the first term, we have only followed the tradition of eminent authors.[13] The lexical anachronism is obvious: to use this term for the Middle Ages, one would say, is to use it too early or too late. The objection is worth making. There's no point in letting this stop us, for historians spend their time using a lexicon and conceptual tools that are anachronistic, projecting categories that are too old or too recent onto the historical reality of a given time. If we are doing it here, Montesquieu did it before us. However, in particular, the explicit use of Aristotle's *Politics* by Peter John Olivi suddenly brings the thought of the fourth century before Christ into the middle of the thirteenth century after Christ. Let us spare ourselves the obvious. Just by trying to write history, one is continually making anachronisms. The most important thing is to make them deliberately.

Therefore, the real problem raised by the use of the word "democratic" lies elsewhere. The term, in our own vocabulary, is intrinsically ambiguous. It designates – as inspired by the history of the ancient Greek cities – a system of government, which Montesquieu describes as one of the subdivisions of the "republican government," and, at the same time, a technical operation, and yet again, a base. One speaks of democratic selection of candidates when everyone potentially has access to a given body; one refers to a democratic governance within a body, no longer taking the base into account, if internal designations and deliberations are backed by freedom of expression, and respect, for the most part, majority rule; one considers it a democratic system of government

---

[13] Gratien de Paris, *Histoire de la fondation* ..., 147, speaks of "the very democratic-looking reaction" brought about by the capitulars of 1239; R. Brooke, *Early Franciscan Government* ..., 131, contrasts the "aristocratic" line of John Parenti with the "democratic" line of Elias.

when, in a territorial grouping set up as a state and once the concept of citizenship has been specified, the source of all power lies in popular sovereignty. The third meaning is the only one that necessarily includes – ideally anyway, considering women's difficulty in winning the right to vote – the two previous ones.

It is evident that the use of "democratic," applied to the Order of Friars Minor, can only be understood in the sense of selection of candidates – and, for convenience, we have substituted above the adjective "popular" – and of method of governance. Let us nevertheless eliminate all risk of confusion among the three meanings of the same word, by even more openly embracing anachronism and value judgment.

"Democracy," according to the quip of Sir Winston Leonard Spencer Churchill, "is the worst of all systems of government with the exception of all the others." If this is true, and if, therefore, the evolution towards such a state may be experienced as a goal and a progression – not without a western centrism as powerful as it is ingenuous – one must also recognize that the same teleological imperative does not have to systematically apply to the forms of life – as democratic as they may be – that are usually called "community" and which, while participating in public activity, fall within the private sphere. It is a distinction that Aristotle establishes in plain language from the very beginning of *Politics*. It is true that one may speak of the base as the democratic operation of a party, an association, a union and – why not? – a religious institution. But the strongest democrats will agree that a particular organization – even within a perfectly democratic system of government – has a right to practice selective recruitment based on opinion, conviction, vocation, abilities, or on any other criteria. They will also agree that each person has the right, if exercised in complete freedom, to give up a certain amount of freedom by agreeing to fit into a given body where the rules of governance may not be democratic ones. It was not a concept that was easily understood and there was spirited discussion on this subject from the eighteenth to the early twentieth century, but, for the most part, the discussion is closed today.

That calls to mind even more clearly – for there is nothing worse than unexpressed value judgments – that, whichever type of democrat we claim to be, nothing justifies our consideration of the restrictions governing acceptance of new members in the Order of Friars Minor as an evil in itself; neither does anything force us to view the progress of the Order's democratic governance as a good in itself. The best we can do is wonder whether or not they were true to the original message, but to do so would require returning to the original intention and speaking not of what it means to be "minor" but of what it means to be "Franciscan" in its strict sense. This amounts to putting a single individual, who was dead at the time when the most decisive developments were taking place, in the position to judge the conduct of thousands of persons – a criterion, it must be admitted, which is not very democratic....

It is a known fact that there were restrictions on new members to the Order. One of the principal grievances of the snobbish Salimbene against Elias is definitely the too-important place that he would have made for the lay brothers in the Order, which was certainly felt by the chronicler and by many of the priests to be an anomaly and a humiliation.[14] Thomas of Eccleston does not fail to note that, after Elias's fall in 1239, his successor Albert of Pisa made the portentous remark that, for the

---

[14] Salimbene, *Cronica*, 143-47 and 232-33.

first time, a minister general had just celebrated Mass.[15] The *Constitutions* of 1239 limited selection of candidates to clerics who had received a university education and emphasized the entrance of lay persons – already at a trickle, as can be imagined – as an exception. A short time later, Haymo of Faversham excluded lay friars from offices that until then they had been able to exercise as equals to the friar priests. Finally, the *Constitutions* of 1260 aimed at rigorously controlling all internal promotion from the lay state to the priesthood. Subsequently, laypersons from a certain background found the answer to their religious requirements in the Third Order permanently instituted in 1289 by *Supra montem* of Nicholas IV, while the Minors themselves – henceforth priests in the majority – surrounded themselves with lay servants, going back to the old ways of the traditional monastic orders.

All of the documents reflect this established fact. In the entire latter part of our study, concerned with normative texts and their commentaries, have we heard about anyone besides popes and masters? We wanted to go through the list of these identical university careers – which, for almost all of them, included the obligatory passage through the Paris *studium* – on purpose, so that the very repetition would speak for itself. Nothing further comes of the remarks put forth by Francis's shadow to John of Bannister; we shall never hear the lay brothers' commentary on the *Rule*. The Order of servants had become the Order of masters, beginning with the servants of servants, whom the ministers should have been, and knowledge may be as formidable an instrument in the abuse of power as violence or money. We have yet to understand exactly how the scholars' works were received. It was to this end that we have always scrupulously cited

---

[15] Thomas of Eccleston, *De adventu*, 13.

the manuscript tradition of the various treatises. At best, it is valuable only as an indication, where chance may play its part. David of Augsburg says that he was really addressing the lay brothers; his commentary is known only through a single witness. What does it matter? By definition his audience would not have been able to read it. On the other hand, what is certain is that the actors of this chain of commentaries knew each other and, in their vast majority, communicated amongst themselves. Then, thanks to a decision of the chapter or of the papacy to which they contributed information, they were able to have an influence on the fate of the multitude.

But isn't it a mistake to confuse the possibility of the presence of lay persons in the Order with "popular" selection of candidates? The *Determinations of Questions Concerning the Rule of the Friars Minor* composed in the 1260s proves – to speak frankly – that the poor had been ousted[16] and, on top of it, gives the reason:

> Certainly we all want to be saved and we cannot forbid anyone the right to beg; however, it is not suitable for us, nor for the Church to receive everyone indiscriminately. It is not suitable for us to do so, since, given that the conditions, qualities and mores of people are different, we would frequently be receiving weaklings [*imbecilles*] who would not be able to endure the austerity of the Order and a crowd of beggars [*pauperes*] who would want to lead this life not for God, but for their own sustenance.[17]

---

[16] A. Rigon, "Frati minori e società locali," in *Francesco d'Assisi e il primo secolo di storia francescana*, 267-68.

[17] *Determinationes...*, 344.

The coincidence – even if it be rough – between the end of popular selection of candidates and a more collective internal governance leaves us uncertain as to what to think. This is even more the case if the comparison is made with other religious institutes that the Minor legislators certainly had in mind. It is very obvious that the Order of Friars Minor cannot claim to represent any sort of reinvention of internal democracy. The pioneers in this area are the Cistercians, the Premonstratensians, and the Trinitarians. The most clear-cut achievement of such a system is to be credited to the Friars Preacher. Now, particularly in the case of the Cistercians or the Preachers, this governance that we would be tempted to call democratic – premature from the viewpoint of comparable institutions – is, from the very beginning, also accompanied by a very exclusive restrictions conderning candidacy.[18] The social and priestly elite of the choir monks in the Order of Citeaux, and the priestly and intellectual elite – and social elite, as well, one would be inclined to think – but we are lacking research on social advancement by education in the eleventh-fifteenth centuries with Dominic's friars.

If one adds that the men of old were sometimes suspicious of elections to the magistracy, seeing them more as the mark of an oligarchic system of government in contrast to a democratic drawing of lots, one may legitimately wonder whether the initial definition should not instead be seriously revised, for the Minors as well, under the following form: the goverrnance becomes aristocratic when the selection of candidates establishes itself as exclusive. Let us push the speculation a bit farther: are not those which we call indirect democracies always a little bit of a combination between a popular base and an oligarchic governance? This is very much

---

[18] D.E. Showalter, *art. cit.*

why Jean-Jacques Rousseau forcefully asserts, in Chapter I of Book II of *The Social Contract*, that "the sovereign power [that is, the people] can only be represented by itself; the power may well be passed on, but not the will." Without it, how is the re-formation – at the very heart of the republican system of government – of certain "nobilities of State" to be avoided?[19]

Here the question comes up of the references directing the institutional development of the Order of Friars Minor. In the Franciscan phase, the meaningful influence was that of the Cistercian model, warmly recommended by the papacy. Beginning in 1239 and under the determining behest of Haymo of Faversham, the assumed model was that of the neighbors of the *studia*, the Friars Preacher. When a Minor chronicler speaks of an election that we would call democratic, he calls it "canonical," since it is in conformity with the canons of the Fourth Lateran Council. We leave to the specialists the task of measuring the earlier influence of ancient Roman law on the development of Church law. The belated sudden emergence of the thought of Aristotle into the discussion, just after the Chapter of Narbonne, has not been neglected, but it would be excessive to grant it any other effect than that of accompanying a corpus and a reflection that are already solidly put together. We cannot completely avoid the question of relationships between the institutional governance of the Friars Minor and the governmental system of the Communes.

In the so-called Franciscan sources, the allusions to a Commune system of government are not so frequent. Giulia Barone discovered one of them in Salimbene's

---

[19] P. Bourdieu, *La noblesse d'État. Grandes écoles et esprit de corps*, Paris, 1989.

writings.[20] Speaking in favor of offices of short duration in the Order, the chronicler of Parma observes:

> We see in these days that in Italy, in the cities, the captains and mayors are changed twice per year and that they render justice very well and fulfill perfectly their task of governing. Indeed, when they arrive, they swear to respect the statutes which were enacted by the wise ones of the city to which they come. In addition, they make use of judges and of advisers who are governed by the law of the elders and whose advice they seek in all things. For, if it is true that "there exist an infinite number of fools," it is also true that "the great number of wise people gives health to the whole earth." If therefore the seculars govern cities well in only a short time, how much more could the religious – who have a *Rule* and the statutes of the elders and their conscience and God before their very eyes – fulfill well their task of governing![21]

Giulia Barone notes how much the remark, which by the way did not have the expected effect, conveys a feeling of the Friar Minor's institutional superiority, who knows his Order to be equipped with a powerful rule in comparison to the Commune's "popular" system of government which he has before him in the second half of the thirteenth century and which therefore must be assumed to be less solidly established, with a less clearly defined governance.[22]

---

[20] G. Barone, "Note sull'organizzazione amministrativa," 59 and 68-70.

[21] Salimbene, *Cronica*, 230.

[22] H. Keller, "Wahlformen und Gemeinschaftsverständnis in den italienischen Stadtkommunen (12./14. Jahrhundert)," in *Wahlen und Wählen im Mittelalter*. Herausgegeben von Reinhard Schneider und

On repeated occasions, soon after the death of Francis of Assisi, friars intervened in a decisive way in the life of the Communes – particularly in those of the Po Valley.[23] Did they take advantage of this to influence the *Statuts* of the Commune, breathing into them something of their institutional practices, of their conception of government? Is there any sign that they were inspired by them to develop their own regulations?

The only known intervention of Anthony in the *Statuts* of Padua, dated March 7, 1231, is a clause in favor of imprisoned debtors.[24] In the "great devotion" – also known as the "Alleluia" – movement, which put the cities of the Po Valley in turmoil from January to November of 1233 under the instigation of preachers from the Friars Minor and Friars Preacher, the friars intervened in the reforms of the Commune's *Statuts* of the various concerned cities.[25] An example is the Minor, Girard of Modena, at Parma. Salimbene wants him to be mayor of the city,[26] even if the allegation is not confirmed in public documentation. The oldest *Statuts* of Parma include forty-four interventions that are explicitly attributed to the Friar Minor and which he must have written from July 15 to September 29, 1233. Augustine Thompson has grouped them together in this way: measures aimed at keeping the civic peace, controlling deportations, protecting widows, minors, and orphans, administering

---

Harald Zimmermann, Vorträge und Forschungen, 37 (Sigmaringen, 1990), 345-74.

[23] P. Evangelisti, "Per uno studio della testualità politica francescana tra XIII e XV secolo. Autori e tipologia delle fonti," *Studi medievali*, 3a ser. 37 (1996): 550.

[24] M. Cusato, *La renonciation ...*, 283.

[25] A. Vauchez, "Une campagne de pacification en Lombardie autour de 1233. L'action politique des Ordres mendiants d'après la réforme des statuts communaux et les accords de paix," *Mélanges d'archéologie et d'histoire*, 78 (1966): 503-49.

[26] Salimbene, *Cronica*, 106.

justice, fighting against heretics, and defending the freedom of the Church. Other additions aim at fighting fornication, adultery, divination, potions, indecency, and blasphemy. Nothing, we see, that has anything to do with the running of the government. The chronicles, for their part, indicate similar decrees in other cities against usury, prostitution, and the display of luxury. Still nothing that resembles a "constitutional" reform.[27]

In his *History*, Thomas, the Archdeacon of Split, relates that in 1238 his city was torn by conflict so violent that the idea came out to adopt a "Latin system of government" – meaning, to resort to government by a mayor. The Friars Minor devoted themselves as active champions of this project, vaunting the merits of such a governmental system, and the temporary magistrate, who by principle was to be from outside the city – this was the condition to enable him to be above the local factions –, was sought in Ancona.[28] The incident is fascinating. It clarifies the role played by the local friars in a difficult political situation – their function as a resource, as public guides in crisis situations, and their concern for internal peace-keeping. The Minors, confident of their "international" network, favor the diffusion and acculturation of the political practices of the Communes of Italy onto the Eastern bank of the Adriatic. The ideal mayor is found in Ancona with the aid of this city of the Marches' own mayor and of a wise local Friar Minor. Yet, beyond this specific context, nothing supports the claim of a closer and more essential link between government

---

[27] A. Thompson, *Predicatori e politica nell'Italia del XIII secolo. La "grande devozione" del 1233*, Fonti e ricerche, 9 (Milan, 1996).

[28] E. Artifoni, "Gli uomini dell'assemblea. L'oratoria civile, i concionatori e i predicatori nella società comunale," in *La predicazione dei frati dalla metà del '200 alla fine del '300. Atti del XXII convegno internazionale, Assisi, 13-15 ottobre 1994* (Spoleto, 1995), 163-64.

of the Friars and a Commune's "mayoral" system of government.

In fact, however, under one variation or another of the governmental system of the Commune such as was flourishing in central and northern Italy in the thirteenth century, examples abound of fruitful exchanges between friars and Communes: the friary was often where the archives were kept, and where assemblies were held, if needed; brothers were in charge of some area or other of the public administration and were involved in external ambassadorships or in internal reconciliations.[29] There are so many indisputable indications of harmony between the Minor Order and civic life, of the extraordinary way that friars settled into the urban reality,[30] without – for all that – its being possible to establish an institutional "contamination" in either direction. Minors and Communes, whether they be "mayoral" or "popular," are objectively contemporary; the two systems – religious and civic – live in symbiosis, each perhaps partaking, in their respective origins, of a same movement of easing the tensions of society and the opening up of the political spectrum; yet, from the standpoint of the principles of their respective governments, each seems to have lived its own life. And when the political context is that of the city-state or of the kingdom, the friars adapt just as well and seek to make themselves the prince's advisers.[31]

In fact, the yardstick against which the "constitutional" norm progressively developed by the Order of Friars Minor should be measured is none other than the range

---

[29] A. Bartoli Langeli, "Comuni e frati minori," in *Il francescanesimo nell'Umbria meridionale nei secoli XIII-XIV. Atti del V convegno di studio, Narni-Amelia-Alviano, 23-25 maggio 1982* (Narni, 1985), 91-9; A. Rigon, *art. cit.*, 273-75.

[30] Id., *ibid.*, 259-81.

[31] P. Evangelisti, *art. cit.*, 549-623.

of institutional options expressed within the Order and – at least this is the belief formed from the studied sources – which were the subject of a real debate. It is not a question of returning to it here in detail, since examples were given throughout the presentation. Some of its essential features nevertheless deserve to be mentioned very briefly.

First, the important years: 1220, 1239, and 1260 mark, at twenty-year intervals, the high points of this reflection, in connection with the situations that occurred.

The beginning of the debate is the least well-informed. It takes place during Francis's lifetime and shows through in the autobiographical accounts, legends, or chronicles; along with the two preserved *Rules*, it left behind only its results and not the written deposit of the opposing positions themselves. The issues – expressed in ancient or modern terms, whichever is desired, and which must almost automatically be put in quotation marks – appear to be the following: the charismatic power of the founder applying itself in a chaotic way to the majority of the brothers, or the oligarchic power of the most educated brothers; a semblance of legislative power as a rubber stamp of the executive, or relative separation of powers and real control of the second by the first; direct democracy, or indirect democracy with the corollary question of representativeness. In the background are the numerical growth of the Order and the mass arrival of the lettered friars. Francis, who feels himself to be sharply attacked, replies paradoxically with his resignation and the more organic relationship that he forms with the Roman See, which has the effect of maintaining an ambiguous situation up to 1226. *Quo elongati* belatedly provides the basic principle of the solution with the reaffirmation of the minister general's power, but it also provides the basis of a very incomplete form of representativeness within the general chapter.

The debate is revived around 1239, in a violent crisis that breaks out regarding Brother Elias's abuse of power. We see traces of it in the chronicles, in the normative measures of the *Constitutions* of 1239 and the allusions to these which were made during Haymo of Faversham's generalate, but we have also preserved one of the opinions put forward in the discussion, with the *Exposition* of the Four Paris Masters. The condemnation of the absolute power of Elias (a former democracy having evolved into a demagogic autocracy) appears unanimous, even if it should not be forgotten that his supporters – and Thomas of Eccleston slides over the fact that he will keep some – were not the most culturally well-placed to make themselves heard. The opposing positions seem to be the following: the first, which is perhaps not unrelated to the writing of the *Anonymous of Perugia* in 1240-1241, is the collective option which prevails in the *Constitutions* of 1239, with a pyramid-shaped structure that draws its legitimacy from the fact that it rests on the base of all the brothers. This is a clear precedence of the legislative over the executive, strictly and doubly controlled by the local elected superiors and the low-ranking friars designated specifically for that purpose. The second, which is expressed in the *Exposition* of the Four Masters and is to inspire in large part Haymo of Faversham's alterations, consists in preserving the same democratic and parliamentary format, while however controlling the system to the benefit of a cultural elite of superiors who set themselves up in a relatively closed system. The two options are in harmony regarding a certain decentralization of power from the center toward the provinces – a center which is henceforth much more Paris than Assisi or Rome. In the background are the marginalization of the lay brothers and the clericalization of the Order.

Some time during the 1250s, the danger that Elias had represented becomes less pronounced, especially since there is no chance that the office of minister general will fall again into the hands of a lay person. The crises at this point are more external than internal, with the violent attacks of the secular masters against the Mendicants at the University of Paris, which have the effect of reuniting the Order of Friars Minor around its fundamental values and its hierarchy. The *Commentary* of Hugh of Digne, claiming to represent a return to Franciscan origins, is the first to dare to extol again the office of minister general. The arrival of Bonaventure at the head of the Order, on February 2, 1257, is therefore the triumphant success of the most brilliant Minor Master of Paris: his election, on the joint suggestion of his retired predecessor John of Parma and Pope Alexander IV is – more than one clan's victory – the elevation of a preferred order. A representative of this cultural elite, the new minister general has the skill to seem not to touch the anti-autocratic *Constitutions* of 1239, yet he still increases the real power of the superiors in general and of the Order's head in particular. From 1239 to 1260, the institutional system evolves no longer by alternating bouts of sudden weakness, but by stratification. Each layer's contribution is adjusted by the one that follows, but is not completely removed. The form of government which results from the *Constitutions* of Narbonne thus reconciles the democratic basis of the *Constitutions* of 1239 – disenfranchising for the local superiors but still effective for the "discreet" friars –, the oligarchic system put in place by Haymo of Faversham's alterations and the monarchism – it would be tempting to say "presidentialism" – of the minister general legitimated by the patriarchal figure of the founder.

Thus, that is the parable on power – roughly summarized and certainly done in a way that is highly

questionable, because it is deliberately very personal –
that the Order of Friars Minor wrote in the days when
it was feeling its way toward its institutional definition.
Francis of Assisi's original negligence had the effect
of inviting his brothers and heirs to unusually careful
thought and of opening up an undeniable area of free
expression with their discussion of ideas. Isn't this – as
unintentional as it may be – one more credit to put down
in the founder's favor?

For, like it or not, what it teaches us is that intuition
only decidedly stands the test of time through the
institution that results from it and that the institution
may have a chance to keep its original spark alive only
when its members, confronted with reality and the
passing of time, are in a position to become – of their
own free will and in their own way – its agents and active
guarantors.

BIBLIOGRAPHY

PRIMARY SOURCES

Actus beati Francisci et sociorum eius. In *Fontes franciscani*. 2085-2219.

Angelo Clareno. *Expositio super Regulam fratrum minorum*. G. Boccali, F. Accrocca and M. Bigaroni, eds. Assisi (Pubblicazioni della Biblioteca francescana, Chiesa nuova, Assisi, 7), 1994.

Anonymus Perusinus. *De inceptione vel fundamento Ordinis*. In *Fontes franciscani*. 1311-1351.

Bonaventure. *Epistola de tribus quaestionibus ad magistrum innominatum*. In *Opera omnia*, 8. Quaracchi, 1898. 331-336.

_____. *Legenda maior s. Francisci*. In *Fontes franciscani*. 777-911.

Bullarium franciscanum romanorum pontificum constitutiones, epistolas ac diplomata continens tribus Ordinibus Minorum, Clarissarum et Poenitentium a seraphico patriarcha sancto Francisco institutis concessa ab illorum exordio ad nostra usque tempora, 1. G.G. Sbaraglia, ed. Rome, 1759.

Burchard d'Ursperg. *Chronicon*. O. Abel and L. Weiland, eds. In *Monumenta Germaniae historica*. Hanover (Scriptores, 23), 1874. 333-383.

Chronica generalium ministrorum Ordinis fratrum minorum. In *Chronica XXIV generalium Ordinis minorum cum pluribus appendicibus inter quas excellit hucusque ineditus Liber de laudibus s. Francisci fr. Bernardi a Bessa.* Quaracchi (Analecta franciscana, 3), 1897. 1-575.

Chronicon Montis Sereni. E. Ehrenfeuchter, ed. In *Monumenta Germaniae historica,* Hanover (Scriptores, 23), 1874. 139-226.

David of Augsbourg. *Expositio Regulae edita a frate David sanctissimo.* E. Lempp, ed. "David von Augsburg: Schriften aus der Handschrift der Münchener Hof- und Staatsbibliothek Cod. lat. 15312 zum erstenmal veröffentlich." *Zeitschrift für Kirchengeschichte* 19 (1899): 345-359. D. Flood. "Die Regelerklärung des Davids von Augsburg." *Franziskanische Studien* 75 (1993): 201-242.

De fratrum minorum Constitutionibus praenarbonensibus. C. Cenci, ed. *Archivum franciscanum historicum* 83 (1990): 50-95.

Definitiones capitulorum generalium Ordinis fratrum minorum, 1260-1282. A.G. Little, ed. *Archivum franciscanum historicum* 7 (1914): 676-682.

Determinationes quaestionum super Regulam fratrum minorum. In Bonaventure, *Opera omnia,* 8. Quaracchi, 1898. 337-374.

"Diffinitiones" capituli generalis o.f.m. narbonensis (1260). F.M. Delorme, ed. *Archivum franciscanum historicum* 3 (1910): 491-504.

Expositio quatuor magistrorum super Regulam fratrum minorum (1241-1242). L. Oliger, ed. Rome, 1950.

Fontes franciscani. E. Menestò and S. Brufani, eds. Assisi (Testi, 2), 1995.

Francis of Assisi. *Admonitiones*. In François d'Assise. *Écrits*. 90-116.

_____. *Canticum fratris Solis vel Laudes creaturarum*. In François d'Assise. *Écrits*. 342-344.

_____. *De vera et perfecta laetitia*. In François d'Assise. *Écrits*. 118-120.

_____. *Epistola ad fideles (recensio posterior)*. In François d'Assise. *Écrits*. 228-242.

_____. *Epistola toti Ordini missa*. In François d'Assise. *Écrits*. 244-254.

_____. *Epistola ad custodes*. In François d'Assise. *Écrits*. 256-258.

_____. *Epistola ad quendam ministrum*. In François d'Assise. *Écrits*. 262-264.

_____. *Regula bullata*. In François d'Assise. *Écrits*. 180-198.

_____. *Regula non bullata*. In François d'Assise. *Écrits*. 122-178.

_____. *Regula pro eremitoriis data*. In François d'Assise. *Écrits*. 200-202.

_____. *Salutatio virtutum*. In François d'Assise. *Écrits*. 270-272.

_____. *Testamentum*. In François d'Assise. *Écrits*. 204-210.

François d'Assise. *Écrits*. T. Desbonnets, J.-F. Godet, T. Matura and D. Vorreux, eds. Paris (Sources chrétiennes, 285), 1981.

Grégoire IX. "Die Bulle *Quo elongati* Papst Gregors IX." H. Grundmann, ed. *Archivum franciscanum historicum* 54 (1961): 20-25.

Histoire des conciles d'après les documents originaux, V, 2. C.-J. Hefele, ed. Paris, 1913.

Hugh of Digne's Rule Commentary. D. Flood, ed. Grottaferrata (Spicilegium bonaventurianum, 14), 1979.

Jacques de Vitry. *Histoire occidentale. Historia occidentalis (Tableau de l'Occident au XIIIe siècle)*. G. Duchet-Suchaux, transl. introd. J. Longère. Paris, 1997.

_____. *Historia occidentalis*. J.F. Hinnebusch, ed. *The Historia occidentalis of Jacques de Vitry*. Fribourg (Spicilegium friburgense, 17), 1972.

_____. *Lettres de Jacques de Vitry (1160/1170-1240) évêque de Saint-Jean-d'Acre*. R.B.C. Huygens, ed. Leyde, 1960.

Jerome. *Epistula* 125 *Ad Rusticum monachum*. In Saint Jérôme. *Lettres*, 7. J. Labourt, ed. Paris, 1961. 114-134.

John of Wales. *Declaratio super Regulam*. In *Speculum Minorum seu firmamentum trium Ordinum....* Venice, 1513. f. 98v-106r.

John Peckham, published under the name of Bonaventure. *Expositio super Regulam fratrum minorum*. In Bonaventure. *Opera omnia*, 8. Quaracchi, 1898. 391-437.

Jordan of Giano. *Chronica fratris Jordani*. H. Boehmer, ed. Paris (Collection d'études et de documents sur l'histoire religieuse et littéraire du Moyen Âge, 6), 1908.

Jourdain de Giano, Thomas d'Eccleston et Salimbene d'Adam. Sur les routes d'Europe. Chroniques traduites et commentées par M.-T. Laureilhe. Paris, 1959.

Julian of Speyer. *Vita s. Francisci*. In *Fontes franciscani*. 1025-1095.

Legenda de passione sancti Verecundi militis et martyris. M. Faloci Pulignani, ed. "S. Francesco e il monastero di S. Verecondo." *Miscellanea francescana* 10 (1906): 6-7.

Legenda Perusina seu Compilatio Assisiensis. In *Fontes franciscani.* 1471-1690.

Legenda trium sociorum. In *Fontes franciscani.* 1373-1445.

Les plus anciens textes de Cîteaux. J. de la Croix Bouton and J.B. Van Damme, eds. Achel (Cîteaux - Commentarii cistercienses - Studia et documenta, 2), 1985.

Pellegrino de Bologne. *Chronicon abbreviatum de successione ministrorum generalium.* A.G. Little, ed. In *Tractatus fr. Thomae vulgo dicti de Eccleston de adventu fratrum minorum in Angliam.* Paris (Collection d'études et de documents sur l'histoire religieuse et littéraire du Moyen Âge, 7), 1909. 141-145.

Peter Olivi's Rule Commentary: Edition and Presentation. D. Flood, ed. Wiesbaden (Veröffentlichungen des Instituts für europäische Geschichte Mainz, 67), 1972.

Saint François d'Assise: Documents, écrits et premières biographies. T. Desbonnets and D. Vorreux, eds. Paris, 1981.

Salimbene. *Cronica.* G. Scalia, ed. Bari, 1966.

Statuta generalia Ordinis edita in capitulis generalibus celebratis Narbonae an. 1260, Assisii an. 1279 atque Parisiis an. 1292. M. Bihl, ed. *Archivum franciscanum historicum* 34 (1941): 37-94 and 284-319.

Thomas of Celano. *Vita prima s. Francisci.* In *Fontes franciscani.* 275-424.

_____. *Vita secunda s. Francisci.* In *Fontes franciscani.* 443-639.

_____. *Tractatus de miraculis*. In *Fontes franciscani*. 643-754.

Thomas of Eccleston. *Tractatus fr. Thomae vulgo dicti de Eccleston de adventu fratrum minorum in Angliam*. A.G. Little, ed. Paris (Collection d'études et de documents sur l'histoire religieuse et littéraire du Moyen Âge, 7), 1909.

Vita ejusdem Gregorii papae IX ex cardinali Aragonio. L.A. Muratori, ed. *Rerum italicarum scriptores*, III, 1. Milan, 1723. 575-587.

SECONDARY SOURCES

Accrocca, F. *Francesco e le sue immagini: Momenti della evoluzione della coscienza storica dei frati minori (secoli XIII-XVI)*. Padua (Centro studi antoniani, 27), 1997.

_____. "Francesco e la sua *Fraternitas*: Caratteri e sviluppi del primo movimento francescano." In F. Accrocca and A. Ciceri. *Francesco e i suoi frati. La Regola non bollata: una regola in cammino*. Milan (Tau, 6), 1998. 9-124.

Alberzoni, M.P. *Francescanesimo a Milano nel duecento*. Milan (Fonti e ricerche, 1), 1991.

Artifoni, E. "Gli uomini dell'assemblea: L'oratoria civile, i concionatori e i predicatori nella società comunale." In *La predicazione dei frati dalla metà del duecento alla fine del trecento*. 141-188.

Barone, G. "Note sull'organizzazione amministrativa e la vita delle province nei primi decenni di storia francescana." In *Studi sul Medioevo cristiano offerti a Raffaelo Morghen per il 90° anniversario dell'Istituto storico italiano (1883-1973)*. Rome (Studi storici, 83-87), 1974. 57-70.

_____. "Frate Elia." *Bullettino dell'Istituto storico italiano per il Medio Evo e Archivio muratoriano* 84 (1974-1975): 88-144.

_____. "Frate Elia: suggestioni da una rilettura." In *I compagni di Francesco e la prima generazione minoritica. Atti del XIX convegno internazionale, Assisi, 17-19 ottobre 1991*. Spoleto, 1992. 59-80.

Bartoli Langeli, A. "La realtà sociale assisana e il patto del 1210." In *Assisi al tempo di san Francesco. Atti del V convegno internazionale, Assisi, 13-16 ottobre 1977*. Assisi, 1978. 271-336.

_____. "Le radici culturali della 'popolarità' francescana." In *Il francescanesimo e il teatro medievale. Atti del convegno nazionale di studi, San Miniato, 8-9-10 ottobre 1982*. Castelfiorentino (Biblioteca della "Miscellanea storica della Valdelsa", 6), 1984. 41-58.

_____. "Comuni e frati minori." In *Il francescanesimo nell'Umbria meridionale nei secoli XIII-XIV. Atti del V convegno di studio, Narni-Amelia-Alviano, 23-25 maggio 1982*. Narni, 1985. 91-99.

Bloch, M. *Apologie pour l'histoire ou métier d'historien*. Paris, 1949.

Boni, A. "Accessibilità indifferenziata (chierici e non-chierici) agli uffici di governo nella Regola francescana." *Apollinaris* 55 (1982): 590-623.

Brooke, R. *Early Franciscan Government: Elias to Bonaventure*. Cambridge, 1959.

Bultot, R. *Christianisme et valeurs humaines: La doctrine du mépris du monde en Occident de saint Ambroise à Innocent III*. Paris, 1963-1964.

Bynum, C.W. *Jesus as Mother: Studies in the Spirituality of the High Middle Ages*. Berkeley-Los Angeles-London, 1982.

Cammarosano, P. *Italia medievale: Struttura e geografia delle fonti scritte*. Rome (Studi superiori NIS, 109, Storia), 1991.

Casagrande, G. "Un Ordine per i laici: Penitenza e Penitenti nel Duecento." In *Francesco d'Assisi e il primo secolo di storia francescana*. 237-255.

Ciceri, A. "La *Regula non bullata*: Saggio storico-critico e analisi testuale." In F. Accrocca and A. Ciceri. *Francesco e i suoi frati: La Regola non bullata: una regola in cammino*. Milan (Tau, 6), 1998. 125-264.

Conti, M., Mayeur M. and Odoardi G. "Ministro." In *Dizionario degli Istituti di perfezione*, 5. Rome, 1978. Col. 1363-1369.

Cusato, M. *La renonciation au pouvoir chez les frères mineurs au 13e siècle*. A. Vauchez, dir. (Diss. PhD., Université de Paris IV – Sorbonne,1991.

D'Acunto, N. "Il vescovo Guido oppure i vescovi Guido? Cronotassi episcopale assisana e fonti francescane." In *Mélanges de l'École française de Rome: Moyen Âge* 108 (1996): 479-524.

Dalarun, J. *Francesco, un passaggio: Donna e donne negli scritti e nelle leggende di Francesco d'Assisi*. Rome (I libri di Viella, 2), 1994.

_____. "Francesco nei sermoni: agiografia e predicazione." In *La predicazione dei frati dalla metà del duecento alla fine del trecento*. 337-404.

_____. *Francis of Assisi and the Feminine*. St. Bonaventure, 2006.

_____. *François d'Assise, un passage: Femmes et féminité dans les écrits et les légendes franciscaines.* Arles, 1997.

_____. "La dernière volonté de saint François. Hommage à Raoul Manselli." *Bullettino dell'Istituto storico italiano per il Medio Evo e Archivio muratoriano* 98 (1986): 161-199.

_____. *La Malavventura di Francesco d'Assisi. Per un uso storico delle leggende francescane.* Milan (Fonti e ricerche, 10), 1996.

_____. "La mort des saints fondateurs, de Martin à François." In *Les fonctions des saints dans le monde occidental (IIIe-XIIIe siècle). Actes du colloque organisé par l'École française de Rome avec le concours de l'Université de Rome "La Sapienza", Rome, 27-29 octobre 1988.* Rome (Collection de l'École française de Rome, 149), 1991. 193-215.

_____. "Les maisons des frères: matériaux et symbolique des premiers couvents franciscains." In *Le village médiéval et son environnement: Mélanges en l'honneur de Jean-Marie Pesez.* Paris, 1997. 75-95.

_____. "Postfazione." In F. Accrocca. *Francesco e le sue immagini: Momenti della evoluzione della coscienza storica dei frati minori (secoli XIII-XVI).* Padua (Centro studi antoniani, 27), 1997. 233-252.

_____. "Pouvoir et autorité dans l'Ordre double de Fontevraud." In *Les religieuses dans le cloître et dans le monde.* 335-351.

_____. *The Misadventure of Francis of Assisi: Toward a Historical Use of the Franciscan Legends.* St. Bonaventure, 2002.

Dalla "sequela Christi" di Francesco d'Assisi all'apologia della povertà. Atti del XVIII convegno internazionale, Assisi, 18-20 ottobre 1990. Spoleto, 1991.

Dal Pino, F. "Formazione degli Eremiti di sant'Agostino e loro insediamenti nella Terraferma veneta e a Venezia." In *Gli Agostiniani a Venezia e la chiesa di S. Stefano. Atti della giornata di studio nel V centenario della dedicazione della chiesa di Santo Stefano, Venezia, 10 novembre 1995.* Venice, 1997. 27-85.

Desbonnets, T. *De l'intuition à l'institution: Les franciscains.* Paris, 1983; English transl., *From Intuition to Institution: The Franciscans.* Chicago, 1988.

Dubois, J. "Ordo." In *Dizionario degli Istituti di Perfezione,* 6. Rome, 1980. Col. 806-820.

Duby, G. *Les trois ordres ou l'imaginaire du féodalisme.* Paris, 1978.

Édouard d'Alençon. "Saint François a-t-il existé?." *Études franciscaines* 15 (1906): 481-495.

Evangelisti, P. "Per uno studio della testualità politica francescana tra XIII e XV secolo. Autori e tipologia delle fonti." *Studi medievali,* 3a ser. 37 (1996): 549-623.

Flood, D. *Francis of Assisi and the Franciscan Movement.* Quezon City (Philippines), 1989.

_____. *Hugh of Digne's Rule Commentary.* Grottaferrata (Spicilegium bonaventurianum, 14), 1979.

_____. *Peter Olivi's Rule Commentary: Edition and Presentation.* Wiesbaden (Veröffentlichungen des Instituts für europäische Geschichte Mainz, 67), 1972.

_____. "Pierre Jean Olivi et la Règle franciscaine." In *Franciscains d'Oc: les "Spirituels" (1280-1325).*

Toulouse (Cahiers de Fanjeaux, 10), 1975. 139-154.

_____. "The Genesis of the Rule." In D. Flood and T. Matura, *The Birth of a Movement: A Study of the First Rule of St. Francis*. Chicago, 1975. 3-56.

_____. "The Order's Masters Franciscan Institutions from 1226 to 1280." In *Dalla "sequela Christi" di Francesco d'Assisi all'apologia della povertà*. 41-78.

_____. "The Politics of the *Quo elongati*." *Laurentianum* 29 (1988): 370-385.

Francesco d'Assisi e il primo secolo di storia francescana. Turin (Biblioteca Einaudi, 1), 1997.

Frugoni, A. *Arnaldo da Brescia nelle fonti del sec. XII*, Rome (Studi storici, 8-9), 1954.

Garzena, C. *Terra fidelis manet: Humilitas e servitium nel "Cantico di frate Sole"*. Florence (Saggi di "Lettere italiane", 50), 1997.

Gratien de Paris. *Histoire de la fondation et de l'évolution de l'Ordre des frères mineurs au XIIIe siècle*. New edition by Mariano d'Alatri and S. Gieben. Rome (Bibliotheca seraphico-capuccina, 29), 1982.

Guyotjeannin, O. *Salimbene de Adam: un chroniqueur franciscain*. Turnhout, 1995.

Keller, H. "Wahlformen und Gemeinschaftsverständnis in den italienischen Stadtkommunen (12./14. Jahrhundert)." In *Wahlen und Wählen im Mittelalter:* Herausgegeben von Reinhard Schneider und Harald Zimmermann (Vorträge und Forschungen, 37). Sigmaringen, 1990. 345-374.

Lambert, M.D. *Franciscan Poverty: The Doctrine of the Absolute Poverty of Christ and the Apostles in the Franciscan Order (1210-1323)*. St. Bonaventure, 1998.

Lambertini, R. *Apologia e crescita dell'identità francescana (1255-1279)*. Rome (Nuovi Studi storici, 4), 1990.

Le Goff, J. "Le vocabulaire des catégories sociales chez saint François d'Assise et ses biographes du XIIIe siècle." In *Ordres et classes: Colloque d'histoire sociale, Saint-Cloud 24-25 mai 1967*. D. Roche and C.E. Labrousse, eds. Paris-La Haye, 1973. 93-123.

Lesage, G. "Capitolo." In *Dizionario degli Istituti di perfezione*, 2. Rome, 1975. Col. 166-176.

Les mouvances laïques des Ordres religieux. Actes du troisième colloque international du C.E.R.C.O.R. en collaboration avec le Centre international d'études romanes, Tournus, 17-20 juin 1992. Saint-Étienne, 1996.

Maccarrone, M. *"Vicarius Christi": Storia del titolo papale*. Rome, 1952.

Manselli, R. *S. Francesco d'Assisi*. Rome (Biblioteca di cultura, 182), 1980; English transl., *Saint Francis of Assisi*. Chicago, 1988.

Marinus a Neukirchen, *De capitulo generali in primo Ordine seraphico*, Rome (Bibliotheca seraphico-capuccina, 12), 1952.

Merlo, G.G. *Forme di religiosità nell'Italia occidentale dei secoli XII e XIII*. Verceil-Cuneo, 1997.

_____. *Intorno a frate Francesco: Quattro studi*. Milan (Presenza di san Francesco, 39), 1993.

_____. "Storia di frate Francesco e dell'Ordine dei Minori." In *Francesco d'Assisi e il primo secolo di storia francescana*. 3-32.

_____. *Tra eremo e città: Studi su Francesco d'Assisi e sul francescanesimo*. Assisi (Saggi, 2), 1991.

Miccoli, G. *Francesco d'Assisi: Realtà e memoria di un'esperienza cristiana*. Turin, 1991.

_____. "Gli scritti di Francesco." In *Francesco d'Assisi e il primo secolo di storia francescana*. 35-69.

_____. *Il Testamento di san Francesco*. Magnano, 1984; French transl., *Le Testament de saint François*. Paris, 1996.

_____. "La storia religiosa." In *Storia d'Italia*, dir. R. Romano and C. Vivanti, II. *Dalla caduta dell'Impero romano al secolo XVIII*, 1, Turin, 1974. 431-1079.

_____. "Un'esperienza cristiana tra Vangelo e istituzione." In *Dalla "sequela Christi" di Francesco d'Assisi all'apologia della povertà*. 3-40; English transl., "A Christian Experience between Gospel and Institution." *Greyfriars Review* 11 (1997): 113-141.

Moorman, J. *A History of the Franciscan Order from its Origins to the Year 1517*. Oxford, 1968.

_____. *Medieval Franciscan Houses*. St. Bonaventure, 1983.

Moulin, L. *La vie quotidienne des religieux au Moyen Âge, Xe-XVe siècle*. Paris, 1978.

_____. "*Sanior et maior pars*: Note sur l'évolution des techniques électorales dans les Ordres religieux du VIe au XIIIe siècle." *Revue historique de droit français et étranger* 36 (1958): 368-397 and 491-529.

Nimmo, D. *Reform and Division in the Franciscan Order from Saint Francis to the Foundation of the Capuchins*. Rome (Bibliotheca seraphico-capuccina, 33), 1987.

Pellegrini, L. *Insediamenti francescani nell'Italia del Duecento*. Rome, 1984.

_____. "Introduzione." In San Bonaventura, *Opusculi francescani/1*. Rome (Sancti Bonaventurae Opera, 14/1), 1993. 7-77.

_____. "I quadri e i tempi dell'espansione dell'Ordine." In *Francesco d'Assisi e il primo secolo di storia francescana*. 166-201.

_____. "La 'Vie de saint François d'Assise' e gli studi francescani tra impegno critico e tensione ideologica." In *Francesco d'Assisi attesa dell'ecumenismo: Paul Sabatier e la sua "Vita di s. Francesco" cent'anni dopo* (= *Studi ecumenici*, 12), 1994, 11-30.

Piazza, A. *I frati e il convento di San Francesco di Pinerolo (1248-1400)*. Pinerolo (Studi pinerolesi, 1), 1993.

Potestà, G.L. "Maestri e dottrine nel XIII secolo." In *Francesco d'Assisi e il primo secolo di storia francescana*. 307-336.

La predicazione dei frati dalla metà del duecento alla fine del trecento. Atti del XXII convegno internazionale, Assisi, 13-15 ottobre 1994. Spoleto, 1995.

Les religieuses dans le cloître et dans le monde. Actes du 2e colloque international du C.E.R.C.O.R. Poitiers, 19 septembre-2 octobre 1988. Saint-Étienne, 1994.

Rigon, A. "Frati minori e società locali." In *Francesco d'Assisi e il primo secolo di storia francescana*. 267-268.

Romano, S. "La morte di Francesco: Fonti francescane e storia dell'Ordine nella basilica di S. Francesco ad Assisi." *Zeitschrift für Kunstgeschichte* 61 (1998): 339-368.

Rubellin, M. "Au temps où Valdès n'était pas hérétique: hypothèses sur le rôle de Valdès de Lyon (1170-1183)." In *Inventer l'hérésie? Discours polémiques et pouvoirs avant l'Inquisition*. M. Zerner, Ed. (Collection du Centre d'études médiévales de Nice, 2), 1998. 193-218.

Rusconi, R. *"Clerici secundum alios clericos*: Francesco d'Assisi e l'istituzione ecclesiastica." In *Frate Francesco d'Assisi. Atti del XXI convegno internazionale, Assisi, 14-16 ottobre 1993.* Spoleto, 1994. 71-100.

Sabatier, P. *Vie de s. François d'Assise.* Paris, 1894.

Sayers, J. *Innocent III: Leader of Europe 1198-1216.* London-New York, 1994.

Schmitt, C. "I vicari dell'Ordine francescano da Pietro Cattani a frate Elia." In *Francesco d'Assisi e francescanesimo dal 1216 al 1226. Atti del IV convegno internazionale, Assisi, 15-17 ottobre 1976.* Assisi, 1977. 235-263.

Showalter, D.E. "The Business of Salvation: Authority and Representation in the Thirteenth-Century Dominican Order." *The Catholical Historical Review* 58 (1973): 556-574.

Sisto, A. *Figure del primo francescanesimo in Provenza: Ugo e Douceline di Digne.* Florence (Biblioteca della Rivista di storia e letteratura religiosa. Studi e Testi, 3), 1971.

Tabarroni, A. "La regola francescana tra autenticità ed autenticazione." In *Dalla "sequela Christi" di Francesco d'Assisi all'apologia della povertà.* 79-122.

Thompson, A. *Predicatori e politica nell'Italia del XIII secolo: La "grande devozione" del 1233.* Milan (Fonti e ricerche, 9), 1996.

Thomson, W.R. "Checklist of Papal Letters relating to the Three Orders of St. Francis: Innocent III – Alexander IV." *Archivum franciscanum historicum* 64 (1971): 367-580.

_____. "The Earliest Cardinal-Protectors of the Franciscan Order: a Study in Administrative History, 1210-1261." *Studies in Medieval and Renaissance History* 9 (1972): 39-52.

Toubert, P. *Histoire et réforme ecclésiastique en Italie au XIe et au XIIe siècles. A propos de deux études récentes. Revue des études italiennes*, n.s. 8 (1961): 58-71.

Varanini, G.M. "Per la storia dei Minori a Verona nel Duecento." In *Minoritismo e centri veneti del Duecento*, G. Cracco, dir. Trento (Studi e testi, 7), 1983. 92-126.

Vauchez, A. "François d'Assise." In *Au temps du renouveau évangélique, 1054-1274*, A. Vauchez, dir. Paris (Histoire des saints et de la sainteté chrétienne, 6), 1986. 143-158.

_____. "Une campagne de pacification en Lombardie autour de 1233: L'action politique des Ordres mendiants d'après la réforme des statuts communaux et les accords de paix." *Mélanges d'archéologie et d'histoire* 78 (1966): 503-549.

Index of Persons and Places

2013.09.23   35.00 (27.25)